PRAISE FOR PETER ECONOMY'S
WAIT, I'M THE BOSS?!?

"This book is for those who aspire to be managers, who are new managers, or who want a refresher. The conversational tone makes the book easy to read, and it is great as a reference guide to keep on the shelf."

—*Booklist*

"A complete guide for training new managers or a refresher for established ones. Every person promoted to a management position should be given a copy of this informative guide."

—*Library Journal*

WAIT, I'M
WORKING WITH
WHO?!?

WAIT, I'M WORKING WITH WHO?!?

THE ESSENTIAL GUIDE TO DEALING WITH
Difficult Coworkers, Annoying Managers, and Other Toxic Personalities

---

PETER ECONOMY

CAREER
PRESS

This edition first published in 2021 by Career Press, an imprint of
Red Wheel/Weiser, LLC
With offices at:
65 Parker Street, Suite 7
Newburyport, MA 01950
www.careerpress.com
www.redwheelweiser.com

ISBN: 978-1-63265-185-3
Library of Congress Cataloging-in-Publication Data available upon
request.

Cover design by Kathryn Sky-Peck
Cover illustration by iStock
Interior by Maureen Forys, Happenstance Type-O-Rama
Typeset in Crimson Pro, Trade Gothic, and Amatic

Printed in the United States of America
IBI
10   9   8   7   6   5   4   3   2   1

To Dandi

CONTENTS

INTRODUCTION

W ho hasn't had to deal with a jerk at work? Whether it's a toxic team member who loves nothing better than to suck the life and excitement out of her colleagues, or a bad boss who causes his employees to constantly dream of telling him to "Take this job and shove it!" or the difficult coworker who isn't happy unless the office is filled with mayhem and drama, we've all had to deal with people on the job we would rather not.

And more than just an annoyance for the people around them, jerks create all kinds of problems for the organizations in which they work. Research shows, for example, that three out of four employees say that dealing with their boss is the worst and most stressful part of their job, and two-thirds say they would happily take a new boss over a pay raise.[1] Not only that, but when it comes to the seventy-three million them in the U.S., a Gallup report says that 21 percent of millennials changed jobs within the past year, and 60 percent of them are open to a new job opportunity.[2]

Why? In many cases because they are tired of working for and with a bunch of jerks.

So, if you can't get these mean, toxic, and lazy people out of your life (you probably need that job, after all, with the paycheck every two weeks and healthcare and other benefits), what can you do to neutralize the negative effect they have on you and your coworkers? Fortunately, the answer to that question is plenty!

This book is the essential guide to identifying and dealing with jerks at work, including bad bosses, troublemaking coworkers, lazy and time-sucking team members, and toxic people of all sorts. As you'll soon see, this book is divided into two parts.

The first part considers the negative impact that jerks have on the workplace—the productivity lost, the employees who quit, the people whose hopes are forever tarnished—and a catalog of sixteen specific species of jerks at work. I suspect that you'll immediately recognize every single one of these sixteen different kinds of jerks.

The second part focuses on eight strategies for dealing with jerks at work—whether you're an employee or a manager. The information and strategies in these chapters will be immediately actionable and profoundly helpful—providing you with the tools you need to counter the jerks in your workplace and anywhere else you might encounter them (believe me—they're *everywhere*).

Based on proven-effective techniques and the latest research and advice of workplace experts, *Wait, I'm Working with Who?!?* provides you with detailed and unambiguous advice on how to deal with and neutralize the negative people in your work life. And, as a special bonus, the advice in this book is just as applicable and effective for life outside of work as it is in it, so you're really getting two books in one.

One note: I have created a series of case studies throughout the book that illustrate common situations we all find ourselves in with toxic people at work. While drawn from my personal experience, they are completely fictional.

My hope is that you'll learn strategies for dealing with toxic people in your life—wherever you may find them. And that, if you're sometimes a jerk at work, you'll recognize that fact and find less-toxic ways to behave. Awareness is a powerful thing, and once you see the toxic people in your life for who they truly are, you can neutralize the impact they have on you and on the people around you.

So, it's time to get to work.

PART I

A FIELD GUIDE TO JERKS AT WORK

*I am thankful for all the difficult
people in my life.
They have shown me exactly
who I don't want to be.*

—ANONYMOUS

Taking on the jerks at work—whether you're an employee, supervisor, manager, or executive—requires first gaining an understanding of the true extent of the problem and its negative effects on you, and then being able to identify the most common jerks in your organization. In this Part, we'll explore the negative impact toxic people have on the workplace and the most common jerks you're likely to encounter on the job. Topics include:

- Revealing the tremendous negative impact of jerks at work

- Understanding the problem of bad bosses

- Cataloging the sixteen most common types of jerks at work—who they are, what they do, and how to identify them

- Assessing the toxicity of coworkers—and yourself

1

THE HUGELY NEGATIVE
IMPACT OF JERKS AT WORK

When dealing with people, remember you are
not dealing with creatures of logic,
but creatures of emotion.

—DALE CARNEGIE

I'm sure all of us have a work story that goes something like this...

It was my first day at a new job. I was excited, wide-eyed, and optimistic about the opportunity and the super impressive people I was certain I would be working with. Dressed in a blue blazer, a button-down shirt, and khakis, I jubilantly walked into the office and introduced myself to everyone I passed by. My boss led me to my new office, and as I got settled in and read through the new employee pamphlet (actually, more like a book than a pamphlet), I heard a voice from the doorway say, "Hi."

I turned around, and the woman who worked a few offices down the hall was grinning at me as she introduced herself. Let's call her Erica. She seemed nice and made me feel welcomed, which were two things any new employee could ever ask for. *Maybe she could be my new work lunch buddy,* I thought to myself. Erica suggested we go to her office to talk, and we did just that—making the short walk down the hall.

As I settled into a guest chair, I couldn't help but catch a glimpse of Erica's computer screen, which had what appeared to be some random website that had nothing to do with work. I didn't think much of it until I visited later and saw the same thing. Every time I caught a glimpse of what Erica was doing, it never appeared to be work related. During staff meetings, our boss would check in with Erica on an assignment and Erica would pretend that she was tirelessly working on it. She would even go so far as to make up the excuse that "It's such a big task for just one person to complete!"

This felt strange and frustrating to me. As her coworker, I saw her slacking every day as she made long phone calls with family and friends, bounced around the internet on her computer, and just generally avoided doing anything remotely related to her job. The biggest personal annoyance was her excessive complaining about work, and how she couldn't wait for the weekend, or how she couldn't wait to leave this "hellhole." *Hellhole? Really??* Yes, most of us are typically excited about the weekend, but there was no need for her to express this to me multiple times every day. And I thought the company we worked at was actually pretty nice—definitely no hellhole.

Regardless, Erica found everything and anything to complain about. She would complain about the coffee machine not functioning properly, our boss assigning her a new task, and she'd complain about everyone in the office and excessively talk about how terrible working at this company was. It was difficult for me to deal with this, especially since I was new to this business and didn't know whether or not to believe her. Not only did it make me annoyed and distracted from doing my own work, but it also made me lose the excitement I had towards the job and company I was working for.

And as I became less excited to go to work and less motivated to do my job and interact with my coworkers, I could feel the energy being sucked right out of me.

I wanted so very badly to get out of this slump, but it was nearly impossible with Erica as my neighbor. We were on the same team and we often interacted as a part of the job. At the time, I had no idea how I could fix this. I began to pick up on subtle things, such as how people seemed to avoid her office at all costs—*was this because she was a bad coworker?*

It wasn't until I had this realization that I began to notice other things. She was never a part of the team because other coworkers didn't want to be around her. They never invited her to lunch or happy hours—nothing that meant they had to spend more time with her.

This was when I decided to make a change. As intimidating as this was since I was so new to the team, I confided in my manager about the issue I had with Erica. My manager informed me that it wasn't the first time someone had brought Erica up with her, which was a huge concern. She apologized for placing me near her as a newbie to the office, and she suggested moving me to an office in a different part of the building. I enthusiastically agreed to the change.

Once I moved, everything changed. Those who worked around me were actually excited, engaged, and productive throughout the day, which in turn made me more excited, engaged, and productive. They were also enthusiastic and happy about their work, which also made me enthusiastic and happy about the work I was doing. I finally felt that same fire that I had felt when I first began working at this company.

In addition, I started to interact with the rest of my coworkers more, and less with Erica. When you spend five days a week in the same office and on the same team as someone, it can be very difficult to avoid them—especially since she often came looking for me. I found this to be extremely hard at first, but it was very necessary for the overall success of the company, as well as my own personal well-being. I didn't realize this at first, but Erica was a toxic coworker who was draining my energy due to her pessimistic nature and unproductive habits.

I wish I could go back in time to tell myself how to deal with my situation better. There's no reason a coworker should make me feel unhappy about my job, and I made a point to never let that happen again. Fortunately, I now know how to address this kind of issue head on. My goal is that you will also learn how to deal with people like

Erica—and other not-so-pleasant types of coworkers. This chapter explores the facts, based on current research and studies, about how bad bosses, toxic co-workers, lazy teammates, and other jerks at work negatively impact the workplace and those around them—and how they affect you, and what you can do about it.

THE PROBLEM: JERKS AT WORK

Just as no two snowflakes are exactly alike, there are many different kinds of jerks that we'll all have the "opportunity" to work with at one point or another during our careers. Many of these people, like my former coworker Erica, can be extremely toxic and rub off on other coworkers in a negative way. Others may only have slight characteristics of being a bad coworker within them, but they poison the workplace—and the people they work with—nonetheless. Small gestures such as leaving early every day or taking excessive sick days can impact the way others feel about their coworkers, their boss, and their company.

Unfortunately, whether we like to admit it or not, many of us have been a bad employee, coworker, or boss at some point in time. Maybe we were late to work one too many times in a week, or we spent too much time scrolling on Facebook when we should have been working on a report or doing some market research, or maybe we even spent most of our day talking to the coworker in the cubicle next to us about non-work-related topics.

We all have a little bit of deviancy within us however much that deviancy might be. If you think of this as a spectrum, we can be anywhere on that spectrum—from 0 percent engaged (nearly impossible) to 100 percent checked out (again, nearly impossible). Someone may be a 1, or a 4, or a 9 on the spectrum of being a bad coworker. However, this doesn't mean they're terrible people who can't be changed—luckily, *anyone* can change for the better. Doing this requires being motivated to change, acknowledging shortcomings, and then learning how to fix them. It is important to be self-aware and understand how you influence those around you.

In research conducted by software and technology authority Better Buys, workers engage in all sorts of bad behaviors at work. Here, according to Better Buys, are the top ten, across a wide variety of industries:.

1. Consistently late: 56%

2. Gossiping behind someone's back: 53.7%

3. Taking a sick day when not sick: 53.2%

4. Yelling at someone: 51%

5. Excessively socializing: 49.2%

6. Taking an unauthorized long lunch break: 42.8%

7. Leaving early without permission: 41.4%

8. Lying to the boss: 41.1%

9. Practicing bad hygiene: 37.4%

10. Working on personal projects at work: 35.3%[3]

As you can imagine, yelling at someone in the office, being consistently late, or lying to the boss can all lead to a hostile, toxic work environment. While reading through this list, do any of your fellow coworkers come to mind? You may even notice actions on this list that you have been guilty of at work as well.

If you relate to one or a few of these behaviors, don't fret. In later chapters, we will go through how you can change these habits within yourself, and how you can learn to deal with coworkers who exhibit them as well.

THE PROBLEM OF BAD BOSSES

If we're going to talk about bad coworkers, then we also need to address another issue in many organizations: bad bosses.

As an employee, chances are you will encounter a bad boss at some point in your career. In fact, research by Gallup shows that bad bosses are the number one reason employees quit their jobs. According to the Gallup report, "Having a bad manager is often a one-two punch: Employees feel miserable while at work, and that misery follows them home, compounding their stress and putting their well-being in peril."[4] In addition, other research reveals that 75 percent of employees say that dealing with their boss is the most stressful part of their job. And, after working for a bad boss, it takes almost two years for people's stress levels to return to a healthy level.[5]

And if you are the boss, it is extremely important to be aware of qualities you exhibit that may be a detriment to your employees. Just because you're the boss doesn't mean you should neglect being self-aware about potential "bad-boss" habits you may have learned over the years. Just like the bad coworker spectrum, there are varying degrees to which you can exhibit potential harmful qualities.

If you're a boss, are you a good one? How do you know?

In 2018, LinkedIn Learning released the results of a survey of almost 3,000 professionals, asking them this question: What is the single most frustrating trait you have experienced in a manager?

Here are the top four traits of bad bosses revealed by the survey:

1. Having expectations that aren't clear or that frequently change: 20%

2. Micromanaging: 12%

3. Being aloof and not involved: 11%

4. Not fostering professional development: 11%

Regarding the number one bad-boss trait above, leadership training expert Elizabeth McLeod says,

> A lack of clear expectations is the root cause of poor performance. Leaders often think they're clear, but the data tells us a different story. Employees need to know why this matters (the purpose) and what good looks like (performance expectations). Show me a leader who says, "I shouldn't have to tell them, it should be obvious," and we'll show you a team that isn't clear.[6]

Luckily, these traits are changeable. Once you acknowledge and realize that you may be prone to specific negative habits, you are able to make that positive change. It may be easy, or it may be difficult. No matter how hard a habit will be to change, it is necessary to do this if you truly want your company and team to succeed. Bad habits won't necessarily change overnight, so be patient with yourself, and believe in the process. Bad bosses often fail to acknowledge their own faults, which ultimately leads to high turnover rates, disgruntled employees, and bad work. Good bosses will want to make this change.

Having a bad boss or bad coworkers in the office we work in, no matter how much or little you work directly with them, can negatively impact your life, personally and professionally. Once you start to pick up on things happening in your office, and how you react to it, you will begin to see the negative impact it is having on you as well as your other coworkers. It is important to do frequent check-ins with yourself and ask questions such as:

- *How does my cubicle neighbor being late to work personally affect me?*

- *Why do I feel on edge every time I speak to this person?*

- *Why do I feel unmotivated and disheartened after I speak to my manager?*

- *How is the overall morale in my office?*

To succeed at work, it's important that you take some time to analyze the reasons you may be feeling the way you do after interacting or working with certain people. Many of us tend to bottle emotions up—especially in a work environment—and this negatively impacts our productivity, passion, and overall happiness.

A prime example of someone who acknowledged the toxic people around him is entrepreneur Ishu Singh. He learned how to deal by ignoring these people in order to continue pursuing his business idea.

Warranties, a set of terms and agreements established by the manufacturer, are used to signal high quality and increase customer trust. But when something you own breaks down, are you, the customer, ever able to successfully locate the manual for the product—originally purchased two years ago? Or do you struggle finding the warranty at a time of urgent repair or replacement?

Ishu Singh can empathize. One day, after trying to fix a broken appliance back in 2017, Singh was unable to locate his warranty, and could not recall any of the product's terms and conditions. He grew frustrated and impatient, unable to understand why it was so difficult to keep track of warranties and user manuals.

Singh, who comes from a family of entrepreneurs, used the experience as motivation to create Innstal, an app that helps you replace traditional hard copies of warranties and manuals with accessible, digital copies. With the click of a button, you can find nearly 1.5 million manuals, curated for all sorts of product users. These documents can either be downloaded or viewed directly on the app, in both text and video format.

Users also have the option to add multiple warranties to the app for different products. After a warranty is claimed through the app, an email is pushed to the manufacturer to process the claim. In the future, the app will also directly link to the manufacturer and further speed up the process of claiming a warranty.

The idea for the Innstal app finally came to fruition in 2019, after it made its formal debut on the Android market.

But this innovative idea and all its success didn't come to Singh overnight. For example, during the early days of Innstal, Singh struggled to fund the project. Despite his family running a successful business back in India, Singh never asked them for any money—instead, he was determined to gather his own resources, working two extra jobs to raise the funds he needed.

But even more concerning, and potentially much more destructive, Singh encountered people who went out of their way to plant seeds of doubt into his mind. They made it clear that they hoped to see Innstal fail. These toxic people with their discouraging comments affected the entrepreneur tremendously, making him question whether they were right and he was wrong.

As it turned out, Ishu Singh was right all along.

Despite the self-doubt and financial hurdles, Singh believed deeply in Innstal and never gave up. Ultimately, Singh's powerful vision of this app became the North Star to guide him along the way, and the driving force of his success.

Like Ishu Singh, you also have the power to overcome these hurdles that may seem like impossible barriers at work. At this point in time, you may not even see them as barriers—you may simply see them as annoying coworkers that everyone has to deal with. Before you move onto the next chapter, please take a few minutes to answer these questions to discover whether or not you work with one or more office jerks:

1. Do you typically feel disheartened or put down by someone at work?

2. Do you lack excitement while working with your team?

3. Do you find yourself trying to avoid certain people at work?

4. Does your boss try to make you or your coworkers look bad in meetings?

5. Do you feel disengaged from your work?

6. Does a coworker or your boss always try to hog the spotlight?

7. Do you ever find yourself looking at the clock on the wall, anxiously wishing you could go home?

8. Is gossip a sport in your organization?

9. Do you have one or more coworkers who try to intimidate you or others?

10. Is there at least one person in your office who is unpleasant to be around?

11. Are you actively looking for another job in a different organization?

12. Do you find yourself complaining about someone or people you work with outside of the office?

13. Have you considered asking your boss to change offices because of a coworker?

14. Do your boss or coworkers ignore you?

15. Do any of your coworkers envy you?

16. Is your boss a control freak?

17. Do you have coworkers who get pleasure from being mean to others?

18. Does your boss think it's *all* about them?

19. Has anyone at work tried to bring your confidence down?

20. Have you skipped a day of work because of a coworker?

21. Have you ever felt the need to lie to a coworker?

22. Are some of your coworkers habitually late to work or do they always leave early?

23. Do you ever try to avoid certain people (or a person) in the office?

24. Have you ever considered quitting your job because of a coworker?

25. Have you ever considered quitting your job because of your boss?

If you answered "Yes" to any of these questions, then guess what? There's a jerk in your life! And if you have more than one yes, then you're working in a toxic workplace.

So, your choice is this: You can find a new job at a new place and quit this toxic workplace. Or . . . you can do something about making your current workplace less toxic and more tolerable. This book is all about how you can turn toxic into terrific!

Now that you know all about the negative impacts of jerks at work, and you've got some idea of the level of toxicity in your own workplace, it's time to get really specific about the sixteen different toxic personalities you are most likely to encounter in your organization.

2

A FIELD GUIDE TO THE SIXTEEN MOST COMMON JERKS AT WORK

Of the billionaires I have known, money just brings out the basic traits in them. If they were jerks before they had money, they are simply jerks with a billion dollars.

—WARREN BUFFETT

Let's get real. Chances are, you've worked with at least one jerk at some point or another during the course of your career. You've probably even worked with more than one. Maybe it was the fry cook who worked the graveyard shift at McDonald's many summers ago. Or maybe someone who works in HR or accounting. Or it might even be your boss (remember: according to Gallup, bad bosses are the number one reason people quit their jobs).

These toxic people can be bad for office morale, your personal sanity, productivity, customer satisfaction, and overall happiness. Over time, you may have noticed that there is more than just one kind of bad coworker—in fact, they come in all sorts of flavors. In this chapter, we take a close look at the sixteen most common types of jerks at work.

As you read through the descriptions of each of these sixteen different personality types, think about which ones you have interacted with throughout your life—or maybe whom you're currently dealing with right now. Ask yourself questions such as:

- How did this person make me feel?

- How did I react to them?

- Did I do anything about the situation?

While going through this list and seeing how the jerks in your own workplace measure up, take some time to look at your own behavior too. Are *you* a jerk at work? We all have a bit of a jerk in us (whether we like to admit it or not), so consider which, if any, of these different characteristics you may be guilty of.

Be honest!

Before you dig into the different personality types, I want to reemphasize one last thing. It is important to look at this as a spectrum—from 100 percent engaged (nearly impossible) to 100 percent checked out (again, nearly impossible). People can have a little bit of a jerk personality type in them, or they can have a lot, or they can even have multiple jerk personality types, all with varying levels of jerkiness depending on the situation. It all depends on the person.

So, without further ado, let's dig into the sixteen different types of jerks at work.

THE SIXTEEN PERSONALITIES OF OFFICE JERKS

Although there is an almost unlimited number of different kinds of jerks at work, in this chapter, we'll focus on sixteen of the most common. This esteemed group includes whiners, people who push meetings off track, drama queens (and kings), those who play the victim, narcissists, people who complain about everyone else, and many more. Are you working with one or more of these jerks? Are *you* a jerk? Either way, the good news is that there's something you can do about that.

Now, let's get started.

The Pessimist

Who are they? Pessimists have the magic ability to see the flaws in just about everything and everyone. They are naturally cynical about any outcome and situation, and there never seems to be a moment of optimism with these types of people. They are the person with a metaphorical rain cloud that hovers above their head everywhere they go, while other coworkers try to dodge getting drizzled on.

Even if your team has never performed better during that last quarter, this person will find something to ruin everyone's high spirits. They're a glass-half-empty kind of person who does not—and may never—understand the glass-half-full mentality that other coworkers may embody. They not only exhibit pessimism in the work that they and their team are doing, but they also may become cynical about specific individuals, which is very toxic.

Case study. Walking into quarterly evaluations with Dave is never something to look forward to. Even in our best sales quarter, he will find something that we as a team—or each of us as individuals—failed at. Dave is our manager, and of course I understand that he's supposed to be critical of our work, but not to the point that it feels like we're all failures—especially when the evaluation numbers show otherwise.

Today was our big, third-quarter evaluation, and we learned that our team sold a total of 245 computer printers, which was more than any team in our company has ever sold in any previous sales quarter. It was huge! As most teams do when they get good news like this, my team of fellow sales associates celebrated this win.

Midway through our celebration, we were suddenly interrupted as our sales manager, Dave, walked into the conference room to start the evaluation. Not once did he congratulate us—he just started out by saying that "Our numbers are nowhere near as high as other printer sales teams at other companies." He continued to point out specific failed sales that occurred throughout the quarter—publicly blaming each sales associate who lost the sale, and thoroughly explaining how each negatively impacted our numbers. He even went as far as to tell us that it was foolish to be celebrating because there was nothing productive about it.

Dave continued to go on with strategy for our next quarter, but also went on to say that it would most likely be impossible for us to achieve our goal due to our team being inadequate. I can honestly say that this hurt to hear. It made me second guess myself. *Was I inadequate? Did we achieve high numbers this quarter just because of luck?* I constantly had to remind myself that Dave had an issue with seeing the positive in *anything,* and that I shouldn't take it personally.

It was hard to work with someone like Dave since he never had anything positive to say. His pessimistic brand of cynicism rubbed off on those he talked to, which ultimately had a profoundly negative impact on the team's morale. When most teams were celebrating their successes, we were left feeling like failures.

Their impact. These negative words and actions from the Pessimist can cause other coworkers to exhibit signs of agitation, unproductivity, nonfulfillment, and lack of excitement. They drain the positive energy from others they work with, creating a negative work environment that can make an impact on the overall morale of the team. This pessimistic mentality is much like a virus that can spread throughout the office. It can cause others to take on the same mentality due to a depletion of positivity.

Since these people are not afraid to speak up when they feel the need to say something, they often come across as confident and all-knowing to others. This pessimistic confidence can sway the mindsets of other coworkers into believing everything that they say. This can be extremely dangerous for the team's mental well-being, and overall happiness in the workplace.

CHARACTERISTICS.

- Glass-half-empty perspective
- Always negative, no matter what
- Asserts their cynical point of view upon others
- Nothing is ever perfect or good enough
- Pessimistic confidence (confident in their negative opinions)
- Typically lacks happiness
- Sometimes they appear to feel like failures themselves
- Uses only negative words and phrases

SURVEY.

1. Are you or a coworker always cynical about things at work?

2. Are you or a coworker talking to other coworkers about reasons your work is worthless, or unsuccessful?

3. Do you or a coworker feel like nothing is good enough?

4. Do you or a coworker never celebrate successes?

5. Do you or a coworker find it hard to see the glass half-full?

If you answered "Yes" to two or more of these questions, you or your coworker are on the spectrum of being the Pessimist.

The Envier

Who are they? Envy, one of the deadliest of sins. It is also one that most of us have been guilty of at some point in our lives; however, some more than others. In the workplace, this sin can be hugely detrimental. This kind of person, known as the Envier, will be resentful and want what you have. Whether it's a job promotion, a "cherry" assignment from the manager, a corner office, or whatever it is you've earned through your own hard work—they will want it.

Unfortunately, envy can escalate to tension and malicious feelings that typically stem from their own insecurities in their work and life. They typically feel as though they unfairly didn't get what they wanted due to a reason outside of their control—it's someone else's fault. They blame the boss for not recognizing the "awesome" job they're doing, they blame their coworker for kissing up to their boss, they blame the world for getting them stuck in this lousy job working for a lousy bunch of people.

They try to feel better by shaming the coworker they're envious of and acting as though the achievement should have been theirs instead. Or they may try a different strategy: belittling the achievement as worthless. Sometimes, they will show self-reflective glory, which means they insert *themselves* as the reason for someone else's accomplishment. This type of person in an organization can create serious friction and unease within the team as a whole.

Case study. My boss called me into her office to give me some good news: I had just been promoted! I had worked at the company for two years and had finally reached my goal of earning a promotion. I exited my boss's office and stepped into a group of my coworkers standing by the door waiting to congratulate me—they had overheard my boss's announcement. I hadn't felt this happy in a long time. It felt so good having the support of my coworkers as well.

After the congratulations, I walked over to my desk, and realized that one of my coworkers, Marissa, hadn't joined in the celebration. She was just sitting at her desk, and quickly looked down as I walked by. From past experiences with her, I knew about her envious tendencies. She would usually confide in me or others about how she should have had the promotion, or she should have had the acclaim from a certain project. Sometimes, I believed her—especially in the first few months after I was originally hired. I thought of her as my friend, and I had hoped she wouldn't be that way with me.

Later that day, I went to the lunchroom, and right as I was about to turn the corner to go in, I heard Marissa talking to two of our coworkers about how I shouldn't have gotten that promotion—I wasn't smart enough, I wasn't good enough, and it was obviously a big mistake. She said that I kissed up to our boss, and that our boss just had a vendetta against her. This should have been *her* promotion.

My heart sank, and I suddenly felt inadequate. *Was it true that I wasn't good enough or smart enough? Was this really just a big mistake?* I also wondered how many people she was telling this to. It made me feel sad. Her envy really impacted me as I went into my new promotion. My self-esteem plummeted, and it was hard for me to feel secure in my new position. Deep down inside, I knew this was all false and just her reaction, but I couldn't help but feel this way.

Their impact. The Envier will often leave team members feeling guilty, unworthy, and uncertain of their accomplishment. This leads to low office morale, discontent, and tension among team members. Many people in the office will feel uneasy around this person, in fear that they will detest them for any accomplishment and persuade others to think the same way of them. This fear is one that alters the way people interact with each other on the team, and the way people react to their own accomplishments.

CHARACTERISTICS.

- Usually feels (and says) they're better than the person they're envious of

- Thinks they deserve whatever they're envious of

- Status and clout are important to this person

- Deep down inside, they do not feel adequate

- Typically superficial

- Shows competitive impulses

- Exhibits self-reflective glory

- Can be angry or hostile towards people they're envious of

SURVEY.

1. Do you or a coworker ever feel envy toward the success of other coworkers?

2. Do you or a coworker refuse to sincerely congratulate other coworkers for their successes?

3. Do you or a coworker find status and clout to be of great importance?

4. Are you or a coworker typically competitive?

5. Can you or a coworker be hostile toward people who have just had successes?

If you answered "Yes" to two or more of these questions, you or your coworker are on the spectrum of being the Envier.

The Intimidator

Who are they? The Intimidator is much like the elementary school bully who used intimidation as a method to get your lunch money. This type of coworker uses intimidation and aggression—or the threat of aggression—to get what they want. They manipulate by threatening and ridiculing their coworkers into doing things for them. The Intimidator has a knack for doing this in a subtle way that leaves their coworker afraid of their perceived power. They may be in a position of leadership because they have bullied their way up the chain of command. This person can often be calm and well-spoken, and their words can sting like daggers.

The Intimidator will use public ridicule and threats in order to maintain control over people. The threats that these people commonly use pertain to destroying careers, and publicly ruining reputations. These are hefty threats that will leave most in fear, which is why many people will succumb to these intimidating ways and do whatever the Intimidator wants.

Case study. Dan was the type of person everyone would actively avoid. Since he was on our team, we of course had to work with him. Other than that, he was definitely one of the last people I'd want to be stuck in our office elevator with.

A few months ago, one of my former coworkers, Steven, fell victim to Dan's ways. Steven was assigned to work with Dan on a project, and every day, he would complain to me about how intimidating it was to work with him. Dan would act like he was greater than Steven, and that this work was beneath him (despite the fact that he had the same job title as Steven).

One day, Steven decided to speak up to Dan, and told him that he was sick of doing all of the work, and that Dan needed to step up and help. Dan's reaction was shocking. In a cool and abrasive demeanor, Dan threatened to tell their boss about something that Steven had said months ago behind our boss's back. He said that he would ruin his career, and that Steven would never be able to get hired in our industry again. Dan's threat to "blacklist" Steven was extremely intimidating, and it made Steven very anxious. Steven loved what he did, and Dan sounded very well connected in the industry. He didn't want to get blacklisted, so he apologized and continued to carry the weight of the project.

After their assignment was complete, Steven decided to leave the company entirely—finding a similar job with a different company. Steven confided in me and told me the reason he left was that he didn't want to do anything that would upset Dan in the future. Steven was afraid of his career in our industry being ruined, so it was easier for him to just play along while he looked for a new job.

Their impact. Intimidation and aggression are very dangerous energies to have in any business, leading to tension, discomfort, and unhappiness within the team. If there is one person (or more) in the office who uses intimidation tactics to get what they want, this will cause a divided dynamic within the team. Coworkers who are victims of the Intimidator's ways will likely not confide in the boss or HR due to the fear that has been ingrained in their minds. The fear instilled in coworkers of this type of person can be paralyzing and directly impact their productivity and happiness in the office. And if the boss doesn't step in to deal with the Intimidator, then employees will start looking for new job opportunities elsewhere.

CHARACTERISTICS.

- Standoffish
- Kisses up to those in higher positions
- Will threaten and/or humiliate for their personal gain
- Manipulative
- Narcissistic tendencies

- Can be very abrasive

- Typically well spoken

- Usually does not have friends, or has few friends

- May portray themselves in a confident, elitist manner

SURVEY.

1. Do you or a coworker threaten and/or humiliate people to get your way?

2. Do you or a coworker tend to use status and power to elevate the fear felt by others?

3. Do you or a coworker lack friendships with others in the office?

4. Do you or a coworker feel elite compared to the rest of the office?

5. Do you or a coworker leverage fear for your own benefit?

If you answered "Yes" to two or more of these questions, you or your coworker are on the spectrum of being the Intimidator.

The Credit Thief

Who are they? This is a person who loves the spotlight. They will do anything to attain accolades for hard work that may not even be theirs. They will take credit from individuals or a team just so they can have praise. When working with a team, they will claim the credit for much—if not all—of the assignment. These people tend to slack off at their own job but continue to pretend as though they have been doing hard work.

The Credit Thief usually ends up getting lots of praise and accolades since many times, the coworker who actually did the work is too afraid to step in and claim their efforts. No matter how collaborative the office is, this person will continue to take credit for work they did not actually do. Much like the Envier, this can stem from insecurities in their own work.

Case Study. I recently noticed my manager engaging in a troubling behavior that she continues whenever she can. She takes credit for the work I actually did. The first time she did it, I thought it would be a one-time thing. But in fact, it has been an every-time thing. It usually goes like this:

We have a huge project that we need to complete by the end of the month. When we are assigned this deadline earlier in the month, my manager and I will put together a game plan, and then we both move forward with our assigned duties. I end up finishing my assigned tasks, and then I check in with her. She makes up some excuse about how she hasn't been able to get to her designated duties because she has been "too tied up" with other assignments. This is her way of saying, "It would be better if you just took over the rest of the assignment."

So, I tell her that I'll just finish this project up so we will be able to present it to the executive team on time. I end up finishing the project, and I send it over to her to read through before we meet with the company executives.

Then, the day of our big presentation comes up. Since she's the manager, she leads the presentation, which leaves me usually saying little to nothing. Throughout the presentation, she uses statements such as "I tracked these numbers" or "I did this," which is completely infuriating to me. She takes all the credit for the hours and hours of work that I did without acknowledging my contributions at all.

The presentation ends, and the executives give my boss a pat on the back for "her" excellent work. Sometimes she will go as far as saying how difficult and time consuming it was to do this assignment, but that she is happy to complete it for the betterment of the company and our customers. I wish I could jump in and say that I was the one who created this entire presentation, did all of the research, and did all of the work—not her. But I don't. This leaves me feeling angry, defeated, and disrespected for the lack of acknowledgement for my work. She refuses to acknowledge the hard work I did to make her look good in front of the company executives.

Their impact. This type of person can cause a lot of deep-seated anger and animosity within those they work with. No one wants to work with the Credit Thief because their efforts are completely taken and undermined by these individuals. It can be emotionally exhausting to have your work credited to someone else. This leaves coworkers unhappy, angry, annoyed, and unmotivated to work if they aren't being credited for everything they accomplish. This adds drama to the office, and it causes friction within the team.

CHARACTERISTICS.

- Typically slacks off

- Confident

- A good liar

- Can be nice and enjoyable to be around, until they steal your credit

- Loves being in the spotlight

- Thrives off of accolades and praise—even if it isn't rightfully theirs

SURVEY.

1. Have you or a coworker lied about accomplishing work that is someone else's?

2. Do you or a coworker tend to slack off and rely on coworkers to do extra work?

3. Do you or a coworker always try to keep the spotlight on yourselves instead of on others?

4. Would you or a coworker lie in order to advance your career?

5. Do you or a coworker thrive off of accolades and praise, even if it's not rightfully yours/ theirs?

If you answered "Yes" to two or more of these questions, you or your coworker are on the spectrum of being the Credit Thief.

The Gossiper

Who are they? This is the person who loves drama, and they will spread any gossip—whether it's true or not—with anyone. These people will turn their back on everyone if the gossip is worth talking about to them. No matter what it's about or who it's about, gossip is worth gossiping. Sometimes these people gossip to hurt a fellow coworker, or sometimes they gossip without knowing the repercussions. Either way, it is harmful and causes a lot of pain and animosity in the team. It can also lead to unnecessary drama that is further amplified by the Gossiper. At minimum, gossip can cause friction within the team, and in the worst cases, gossip can potentially ruin people's careers and reputations.

Case study. Maria was the one who always had the scoop on everyone and everything in the company. I can't say I didn't enjoy hearing juicy gossip from her. It was a nice distraction from the piles of paperwork I had to sort through at my desk. It was a routine: I'd get to the office at around 8:00 a.m., go to my desk to set my bag down and grab my coffee mug, then I'd head to the kitchen to get coffee and hear what the latest office gossip was. It was usually me, Maria, and a few other coworkers.

Maria would talk about anything and everything related to the people in the office—from our boss's marital problems, to our coworker Samantha's potential layoff, to the key customer who was insulted by our sales manager. I never really knew how Maria got this information, but she just somehow was able to.

One day, she was talking about how people in our office were complaining about our recent increase in workload, and I mentioned that it was ridiculous that our boss was giving us so much work. Well, fast forward a few days, and I noticed people starting to interact with me differently. A friend of mine in the office came over to my desk to tell me that Maria was spreading rumors about how I was trying to leave the company. This wasn't true at all! I loved my job, and I felt hurt and afraid that this rumor was being spread.

I decided to go up to Maria and tell her that this rumor was false, and that she needed to fix this. She scoffed and ignored my request. This was hurtful, and I felt so disrespected. I was paranoid that this information would get to my boss and ruin my relationships with my coworkers and company.

Their impact. Gossip can plague an office. The spread of false rumors about coworkers can lead to malicious feelings, tension, unhappiness, and discomfort. People enjoy office gossip—and most everyone gossips. A study by Office Pulse/Captivate found that 72 percent of business professionals reported that they gossip about coworkers or workplace issues while they're at work. The breakdown of gossipers is surprising, with 55 percent of men admitting to gossiping at work, 79 percent of women, 81 percent of millennials, 70 percent of Gen Xers, and 58 percent of baby boomers.[7] Clearly, there's a lot of gossip going on.

Once someone is directly impacted by this gossip, however, it can hugely impact their work and dedication to the team. It can go as far as people becoming disengaged in their work or even quitting their jobs. Gossip is a stressful thing to deal with when you're on the receiving end of it, and it spreads like wildfire. Gossip can impact the way others feel about certain coworkers—whether it's true or not. This causes a disjointed office dynamic that is filled with lots of drama and hurt feelings.

CHARACTERISTICS.

- Likes to talk
- Enjoys being the center of attention
- Lacks remorse for those impacted by their gossip
- Seems like an amicable, social person
- Never includes themselves in the gossip unless it's to benefit them
- Has a hard time keeping their mouth shut
- Loves drama

SURVEY.

1. Do you or a coworker enjoy sparking drama in the office?

2. Do you or a coworker enjoy being the center of attention?

3. Do you or a coworker find it hard not to talk behind coworkers' backs?

4. Do you or a coworker not care about the repercussions of spreading potentially false rumors?

5. Do you or a coworker rarely include yourself in drama?

If you answered "Yes" to two or more of these questions, you or your coworker are on the spectrum of being the Gossiper.

The Lazy One

Who are they? These are people who love to do the bare minimum. They typically procrastinate, and they will manage to get by—but typically at the expense of their coworkers having to pick up their weight. The Lazy Ones can be deceiving because they pretend to be constantly busy and stretched thin, but this is just a facade. This can be misleading to coworkers at first, because they are masters at pretending to be distressed by the amount of work they have. They are able to get people to feel bad for them, cut them slack, or even do their work for them.

This is very similar to the Credit Thief; however, this person does not necessarily take the credit from whoever may have helped them with work. This person typically gets by slacking if the manager or boss does not pay attention to each individual employee properly. This means that the Lazy One can continue their laziness without any expense but their coworkers'.

Case study. At my previous job, I had a coworker on my team who was extremely lazy. It was a miracle he even made it out of bed every morning and to the office. Everything from his slouchy clothing to his lack of actual work accomplished reeked of laziness. Whenever I had to work directly with him, I hated it. I always had to prepare for a busy week working overtime since I knew that I'd be doing the amount of work for two people. I could never count on him to do anything whatsoever. He always had his excuses, but after a certain amount of time, those excuses didn't faze me anymore. I would try to call him out for his lack of productivity, but he never seemed to listen. My words would go in one ear and out the other.

This was extremely frustrating to me. I had brought this up to my boss before, but he never seemed to take it seriously. He mostly just affirmed that I shouldn't be doing this employee's work for him, and that I should just let him do it. I thought it was terrible advice. If I just stopped doing his work, then we would both end up being reprimanded for not having completed our assignment on time. This wasn't worth it to me, so I continued to pick up the unfinished work from my coworker. This just led to more frustration and exhaustion until I ultimately decided to quit my job.

Their impact. No one at work wants to work with the Lazy One. It's known that the coworkers who fall victim to the laziness of this person will end up having to do all of the work. These people are tedious to work with because of their laziness and lack of empathy. They don't care whose shoulders their work weighs on. This can cause a team to be stressed, frustrated, and exhausted by the extra work they have to do—and without any more financial incentive. Working with someone who does minimal work but makes the same amount as you—or more—is very frustrating. This can lead to tension and animosity towards people and the workplace.

CHARACTERISTICS.

- Tired and lazy

- Lacks ambition or motivation

- Doesn't seem to care about anyone else

- Isn't very present

- Does little to no work

- Apathetic towards work and coworkers

- Lacks self-awareness

- Pretends to be working when really not working

SURVEY.

1. Do you or a coworker rely on others to finish unfinished work?

2. Do you or a coworker lack motivation or drive?

3. Are you or a coworker typically not mentally present at work?

4. Do you or a coworker pretend to be working?

5. Do you or a coworker tend to slack off at work?

If you answered "Yes" to two or more of these questions, you or your coworker are on the spectrum of being the Lazy One.

The Micromanager

Who are they? These people are the "helicopter" moms and dads of the office. Typically, this person is in a managerial role, but this is not always the case. The Micromanager constantly hovers over the team, and they feel the need to control everything. If things go in a direction that they don't agree with, they tend to take over the project and complete the work themselves. They lack awareness, and rarely take suggestions from others. They usually lack trust in their fellow coworkers, and fear losing control. Their control is extremely important to them, and if they feel threatened of losing that, they will react by hovering or taking over.

Case study. My manager was a complete hoverer. He would quite literally hover over our desks, constantly asking what we were doing. It was his way of micromanaging. He needed to know exactly what we were doing at any second of the day in order to assess whether we were doing our jobs the way he thought was best. Mind you, his thoughts on what was best were not always best. Sometimes he'd sit in on my team's meeting just to "listen." But the listening would turn into telling us what to do instead.

It was frustrating because we never had any creative control over what we did. Sometimes, it would go as far as him saying that he'd "take a stab at it"—which meant that he would complete the entire project for us. Whenever he did this, it made us feel as though we had not made an impact, and that we were not important assets to our company. It was frustrating to have our voices and ideas stripped away by our manager, never to be heard.

Their impact. Micromanagers often have good intentions and want the company and their coworkers and the people they manage to succeed, but at the expense of their well-being. Their micromanaging tendencies lead to people feeling like no matter what they do, it won't be good enough. Employees will be left feeling unsatisfied by the lack of impact they've made at their job if it is constantly being taken over by someone else. They don't have authority over anything, which can be very frustrating and depressing. This leads to low office morale, low energy, and animosity towards those who are micromanaging.

CHARACTERISTICS.

- Goes out of their way to evaluate what coworkers are doing

- Will take over projects completely

- Typically feels like their coworkers are subordinates who are not as skillful or efficient

- Lacks self-awareness

- Thinks that they are being proactive, but instead they are harming their coworkers

- Overachiever

- Lacks trust

SURVEY.

1. Do you or a coworker constantly assess other coworkers' work ethic and/or ideas?

2. Are you or a coworker prone to completely take over assignments or projects?

3. Do you or a coworker lack trust in those you work with for no plausible reason?

4. Do you or a coworker feel like your/their skills and ideas are superior to the rest of the office?

5. Are you or a coworker an overachiever?

If you answered "Yes" to two or more of these questions, you or your coworker are on the spectrum of being the Micromanager.

The Competitor

Who are they? These people are—as the name suggests—competitive individuals at work, sometimes destructively so. They most likely showed signs of competition at an early age in life, whether it was through sports or academics. They make everything and anything a competition—and usually it's not the fun kind. They consider success being number one, and there is no way they can settle for anything less. Whether it's being the first one in the office every morning, selling the most cars this week, or winning the Employee of the Month award more times than anyone else.

By creating competition in the workplace, they force their coworkers to take part in their ways, getting caught up in competitions that they don't really want to take part in. The Competitor is difficult to work with because no one ever seems to win except for *them*. No matter what, they will find a way to beat you—*always*.

Case study. My coworker Mark always made everything a competition. He had to be the first one to our team meetings so that he could get the best seat, he had to prove that his accomplishment was more impressive than anyone else's, and he had to finish his work the quickest. In short, he had to be first at everything. This grew tiresome for everyone on our team.

At first, I didn't mind it. I always enjoyed some friendly competition to motivate me, but after a while of trying to be on his level, it became exhausting. When we had a deadline, he'd be working on it tirelessly, and he would constantly be checking in on me and my coworkers to see where we were in the process. If we were behind him in work, you could tell that brought him joy, and he would brag about his progress. Once he finished his work—usually well before the deadline—he would make sure the entire office knew all about it. He had no problem announcing to the world that he was in first place—number one.

I sometimes found myself battling in this competition, wearing myself out and stressing that I wouldn't be able to finish my work as quickly as he did, or worrying that our boss would see him as the best employee on our team due to the competition he brought into our office. I know we all work at our own pace, and that quickness does not necessarily equal quality, but it's difficult not to get caught up in his competition. It's toxic.

Their impact. The Competitor wears people out. By making everything a competition, this person forces people to compete, whether they want to or not. Competitive people can stress out other coworkers, causing people to feel as though they aren't working hard enough, or succeeding. They have a tendency of making coworkers feel like they are less great or accomplished, and that their work is not as good as the

Competitor's. This can lead to agitation, low morale, and low confidence at work due to the feeling of defeat.

CHARACTERISTICS.

- Typically intense
- Energetic and excited
- Needs to be number one at everything in order to feel self-worth and satisfaction
- An overachiever
- Will belittle people if they feel that their first-place status is being taken from them
- Lacks sensitivity toward their "competition" (their coworkers)
- Lacks confidence deep down inside, although it may be hard to tell

SURVEY.

1. Do you or a coworker turn anything into a competition?
2. Do you or a coworker feel the need to be number one?
3. Do you or a coworker feel threatened by those who appear to be achieving more?
4. Will you or a coworker belittle someone if they threaten your first-place status?
5. Is how people perceive you important to you or a coworker?

If you answered "Yes" to two or more of these questions, you or your coworker are on the spectrum of being the Competitor.

The Narcissist

Who are they? This person generally feels as though they are better than the rest, and too good for certain work tasks handed to them. They feel the need to be constantly complimented, and to be the center of attention. They typically belittle their coworkers, and they feel superior to the rest—no matter what their job title is.

The Narcissist is someone who cares most about how they are seen by others, and truly believes that they are the smartest, best person in the room. They don't show it, but their narcissism is sometimes due to low self-esteem, and they need to prove to themselves that they are worthy. They do this by acting to the extreme. Other times, this is a side effect that those with superiority complexes have. The Narcissist is often put into leadership roles because of their undying confidence.

Case study. I once had a manager who was a complete narcissist. He would walk into the office like he owned the place. It was so difficult to work with him because he was very hot and cold. He could be nice—but it took me a while to realize that it was manipulative, and any compliment just reflected his own accomplishments.

For example, he would congratulate our team, but he did it in a way that was more a compliment about how *he* led our team to success. He never really asked how we were doing, or even how our day was. He seemed to live in a bubble that only revolved around him. Whenever we had meetings to brainstorm ideas for upcoming projects, he would always trump any idea that anyone else had. If he felt threatened by an idea—typically if others were enthusiastic about a coworker's idea—he would come up with a reason to say that it would never work, or that it was stupid.

He had to be right all the time, and when he was wrong, he managed to find a way to be right. And that usually meant belittling whoever would question him. He cared so much about how he was perceived by other people that he didn't care who he put down in order to attain his ideal standard for himself. It was very difficult to work with him since I never felt like my ideas or voice meant anything to the company. With his self-indulgent ways, he felt that everything surrounded his greatness and that he was the sole reason our company was thriving. This is a very delusional mindset to be in, and it was exhausting to have to witness firsthand.

Their impact. The Narcissist is one of the more frequently seen office jerks. They have varying degrees of negative and positive impact in a company. Since they are very confident about their ability to succeed no matter what, they often make great leaders for a company. The downside is that they are usually extremely self-absorbed, and they are apathetic towards others unless they need something from them, or they get in the Narcissist's way.

It can be very frustrating for coworkers to work with narcissists since this specific type of person belittles and thinks less of everyone else. They also rarely listen to the thoughts or opinions of others, and discredit everyone. This leads to frustration, low office morale, and a lack of confidence and self-worth at work.

CHARACTERISTICS.

- Self-absorbed
- Will talk over people to assert their opinion
- They think that they are the smartest person in the room
- Confident
- They have a hard time listening to other ideas
- They tend to mostly talk about themselves
- They lack humility

SURVEY.

1. Do you or a coworker feel superior to the rest of the office?

2. Do you or a coworker think all other ideas from coworkers are dumb?

3. Do you or a coworker primarily center conversations around yourselves?

4. Are you or a coworker unapologetically confident in yourselves and your work?

5. Do you or a coworker tend to belittle other coworkers?

If you answered "Yes" to two or more of these questions, you or your coworker are on the spectrum of being the Narcissist.

The Complainer

Who are they? These are the crybabies of the office. The Complainer seems to never see the positive side of work or life. They find anything—and *everything*—to complain about. They will verbally express this with their coworkers, which often leads to annoyance and low office morale. They will complain about work tasks, their personal life, anything that has been on their mind, and they will rant to whoever is in ear's reach.

Nothing is ever satisfactory to this person. No matter how big the success is, or how great they're doing at work—they will never feel like anything is good enough, for themselves, or for others. And they are very vocal about it—wearingly so. Typically, they're not passionate about what they are doing at work, and their way of coping with their discontent is by complaining.

Case study. Emily sits next to me in our office. She's fun and nice to have as a friend at work, but there's one thing I can't stand about her. She complains every single day, about every single thing. Her complaining isn't even always about work either. She'll complain about how lazy her husband is, or how her "annoying" best friend from college keeps texting her. I'll be in the middle of working, and I'll hear her sigh, and she'll just start complaining to me—without even acknowledging her. It's very frustrating to me because this usually disrupts my workflow, and her complaining is always negative, which puts me in a negative mindset.

Another thing that she does is complain about people in the office. It's difficult for me because I like our job and the people in the office who she's always complaining about. But when she blows things out of proportion, it's hard for me to remain levelheaded in regard to my opinion of people in the office. If she is saying negative things about our boss or a fellow coworker, I can't help but absorb what she's saying. I try not to, but it's easy to get caught up in her complaining.

Maybe our boss has favorites. Maybe our coworker doesn't actually care about us. Everything she says makes me second guess everything. I've noticed that since she complains about our job so much, I now have a negative viewpoint on our job as well. This has altered my workflow and dedication to our team, since she has tarnished my positive opinions and thrust her own negative opinions into the forefront.

Their impact. Having a Complainer in the office can infect others. Even the most optimistic, content employee can be tainted by the Complainer's negative thoughts regarding the workplace. This can make it difficult for coworkers to feel completely happy at work because the bad attitude of this coworker can rub off on others. This causes less motivation and determination at work, and it causes tension and potential drama within the team.

The Complainer will often complain about different people in the office, which leads to others absorbing their thoughts—and creating a divide within the office. Constant complaining also creates low office morale, which leads to a poor work ethic and unhappiness.

CHARACTERISTICS.

- Complains about everything
- Tends to be social
- Likes to talk
- Lacks self-awareness
- Not passionate about their work
- Usually distracted with their issues
- Bad work ethic

SURVEY.

1. Do you or a coworker complain often?

2. Do you or a coworker lack productivity due to unhappiness in the office?

3. Are you or a coworker discontent with what you're doing at work?

4. Do you or a coworker feel distracted by things that annoy you/them.

5. Are you or a coworker typically negative about most work-related things?

If you answered "Yes" to two or more of these questions, you or your coworker are on the spectrum of being the Complainer.

The Nitpicker

Who are they? This is the type of coworker who is typically a hard worker but can be difficult to work with due to their "know-it-all" mentality. They're perfectionists but often can cause unproductivity and arguments within the team. The Nitpicker is extremely meticulous and will work long hours in order to get anything from font to indentations perfect. They are a great employee in many respects, but for others, it can be very tiresome to work with them.

Working on a project with someone like this will typically lead to long, grueling hours going over little details that may not be necessary in the long run. The Nitpicker typically does not see the end to any project and will keep working up until the deadline. They tend to guilt and convince others into staying overtime with them to work on perfecting projects, which can grow very irritating to coworkers. Sometimes, the Nitpicker may even fail to turn projects and assignments in on time due to their mindset of nothing being perfect enough.

Case study. Whenever we have a big project with a tight deadline, I hope that I don't get assigned to Sam's team. It's not that I don't like Sam; it's just that he makes it nearly impossible to work with him. I was on his team once before, and it was the most physically and emotionally exhausting time of my life.

The final week or so before our project was due, I thought we had it in a good place. I felt confident in the work we had completed, and generally my team thought it looked really great. Then Sam went through everything and came up with page after page of edits that we had to make. I understand the need for edits, but the majority of these edits were superfluous and extreme. He stressed us out about these edits and manipulated us into staying long hours every day until our deadline.

I was barely even able to sleep that week since I would leave at around midnight and get into the office at around 7:00 a.m. My work-life balance was severely altered, and it made me become frustrated and resent my job. Knowing that these edits were completely unnecessary was what made me frustrated, and it made me feel like I was wasting time and losing sleep for no reason. Having a balance between work and my personal life is extremely important to me, so losing this during those weeks leading up to our due date was draining and I became resentful about the intrusion in my life.

Their impact. The Nitpicker can cause exhaustion and low morale due to their perfectionism and idea of nothing being good enough. They can slow progress due to their perfectionism, which can lead to worse results in the long run. This often results in coworkers feeling as though the work they accomplished isn't good enough because the Nitpicker always finds something that "needs" to be fixed. Office morale suffers due to this, and people feel overworked and exhausted. This can lead to unhappiness, a lack of confidence, and tension within the office.

CHARACTERISTICS.

- An overachiever
- A perfectionist

- Has the mentality that nothing is ever good enough
- Willing to work long hours
- Good work ethic
- Doesn't care about other peoples' lives and schedules
- Tends to feel superior and all-knowing

SURVEY.

1. Are you or a coworker very meticulous with details?

2. Will you or a coworker jeopardize your personal life in order to perfect projects at work?

3. Do you or a coworker assume others will also be okay with frequently working overtime for perfection?

4. Do you or a coworker have a great work ethic?

5. Do you or a coworker tend to think that nothing is good enough?

If you answered "Yes" to two or more of these questions, you or your coworker are on the spectrum of being the Nitpicker.

The Malicious One

Who are they? With snide comments under the breath, or painful words spoken behind your back or to your face—these people are just straight-up mean—the Malicious One doesn't care what they say or who they say it to. They will say things to hurt other coworkers' confidence and to intentionally bring people down, creating a toxic work environment in the process.

This kind of person can easily destroy a coworker's mental state and productivity as they release their own internal aggression on others. The Malicious One lacks empathy for anyone, and they don't care how their words can have a negative impact. They feel personal satisfaction by hurting others and ruining confidence because it gives them power.

Case study. When I was new to my job, we had someone in the office who was terribly mean. He had no friends— at least none that we were aware of—and no one enjoyed his presence. If he became annoyed or felt threatened by someone, he would lash out and say something that he knew would hurt the other person deeply. Sometimes he didn't even need a reason to say mean things, he would just say it.

It seemed as though he got a tremendous amount of enjoyment by hurting the feelings of his coworkers. He would make negative comments about their appearance, quality of work, personal life, and everything in between. If he became frustrated by someone's work, he would call out their incompetence and point out other ways they were incompetent. He went above and beyond to remember details, mistakes, and flaws about people so that he could use them when the time came. This made working with him really unsettling.

I never felt fully comfortable being in the office with him because I was afraid that I would be the next victim subject to his ridicule. This gave me anxiety, and my productivity declined because I was always worrying about what he would say to me and when he would say it. His words hurt, and it was hard to recover from that.

Eventually, our boss realized the negative effect this toxic person was having on his coworkers and he was fired. After that, I finally felt comfortable at work for the first time ever. The entire atmosphere became more relaxed and enjoyable, and we all became more dedicated to our jobs rather than constantly being distracted by our hurt feelings - or wondering what bad things he would say to us next.

Their impact. With the presence of the Malicious One in a workplace, there are bound to be hurt feelings and coworkers who feel threatened and unsafe. When the Malicious One is mean to a coworker, the coworker is left mentally distraught, which leads to distraction, anger, low morale, low self-esteem, and reduced productivity. This can spread throughout the office, leaving people feeling insecure, unsafe, and unhappy in this work environment. The Malicious One is not a positive force within the office, and almost always causes more harm than good.

CHARACTERISTICS.

- Can be standoffish
- Feels superior to others
- Usually very aggressive

- Lacks morality and kindness
- Isn't afraid to say what they're thinking
- Is straight-up mean
- Self-absorbed

SURVEY.

1. Do you or a coworker enjoy being mean to others?

2. Are you or a coworker unafraid to say whatever is on your mind, no matter who it may hurt?

3. Do you or a coworker tend to feel superior to others?

4. Are you or a coworker generally an aggressive person?

5. Do you or a coworker rarely—or never—say nice things about other people?

If you answered "Yes" to two or more of these questions, you or your coworker are on the spectrum of being the Malicious One.

The Backstabber

Who are they? As the name indicates, this kind of toxic person has no problem stabbing you in the back at work (metaphorically, of course, not literally). The Backstabber often comes across as a trustworthy person, making a coworker feel comfortable to divulge personal information. However, if the Backstabber feels it will benefit them, they will divulge this personal information in order to hurt their fellow coworker.

In addition, if the Backstabber feels threatened, they will be quick to call out coworkers in order to cast the blame on someone else. They are not afraid of making enemies for the benefit of their needs, and they will do anything to get what they want. This is done by undermining their coworkers in different ways, such as divulging secrets, lying about people, and accusing people of doing certain things—often things they had nothing to do with.

Case study. My coworker Katie and I were up for the same promotion; however, there was only one promotion that our boss could give out. We had talked about this, and we were both excited about the potential, but agreed that we'd be happy no matter the outcome. We both respected each other and knew that either of us would be great for the promotion. Of course, I wanted it, but I was content knowing that my friend equally deserved this.

To get the promotion, we each had one-on-one meetings with our boss. Katie's one-on-one was before mine, and I wished her good luck. She smiled at me nervously and excitedly said, "You too!" I anxiously waited at my desk, periodically looking over at my boss's office. Finally, it was my turn. Katie walked out and gave me an encouraging thumbs up as I walked into the office. I sat in the leather chair across from my boss. She explained the promotion, and that I was eligible for this but she wanted to make sure she was making the right decision by checking in on Katie and me first.

The conversation was going well, although I could sense that something was distracting her. She then said, "I recently found out that you've been telling people how unhappy you are at the office, and that you want to quit the company entirely. If this is true, I do not feel comfortable giving you a promotion knowing that you are planning to quit once a better opportunity comes your way."

My heart sank. The only person I told that to was Katie. There's no way she could have told our boss, could she? Was this Katie's way of getting the promotion? Was this her tactic all along—to backstab me? This was embarrassing, and I didn't know how to recover from this. I couldn't lie to my boss that I didn't say those words, although I desperately wanted to. My relationship with Katie was never the same. Neither of us ended up getting promoted.

Their impact. The Backstabber will sneak up on coworkers when they least expect it. The consequences of their actions can negatively affect the coworkers who have fallen victim in an assortment of different ways. Careers can be ruined, promotions lost, reputations damaged, and the Backstabber can turn people against one another—causing all sorts of turmoil in their toxic wake. All of this causes a lack of trust, low morale, tension, and unease in the office.

CHARACTERISTICS.

- Can seem friendly at first
- Will tell people confidential information about others in order to benefit them

- Very attentive
- Can show competitive signs
- Lacks empathy towards others
- Thinks they are deserving of all things

SURVEY.

1. Have you or a coworker used confidential information to benefit your/their career?

2. Are you or a coworker okay with divulging someone's secrets?

3. Are you or a coworker considerably competitive?

4. Do you or a coworker not care much for your friends' well-being?

5. Do you or a coworker put your needs before anyone else's?

If you answered "Yes" to two or more of these questions, you or your coworker are on the spectrum of being the Backstabber.

The Non-Responder

Who are they? Good luck getting an email response from this type of person. In the middle of a deadline, the Non-Responder is a difficult person to work with. No matter how pressing your question or request may be, this person will not respond. If they do respond, it is typically in a very short manner that may not even answer your question.

Sometimes the Non-Responder lacks self-awareness, and does not realize that their non-responsive ways can be detrimental to others' work. Meanwhile, there are other types of Non-Responders who do this intentionally in order to hurt their coworkers out of spite or self-gain.

Case study. My manager Cameron became a huge frustration for me. Instead of being a support, answering questions, and guiding me in the right direction for my work (as a good boss should), he was very non-responsive. At first, I would brush off his lack of response, thinking it was just because he was busy with something else. Sometimes he would respond back a day or two later, and in a short manner. His emails were cold, and they were only about a sentence or two long.

I didn't want to take this personally, but it was hard not to. I wasn't sure whether I was annoying him with my questions or what. I became very self-conscious about asking him questions, which resulted in me asking few to none. This really impacted the quality of my work. I would be working on assignments, and with no clear direction. I knew that this work didn't reflect my actual capabilities, but I also didn't want my boss to dislike me because I was annoying him with my questions.

On a more recent assignment, I had an urgent question that was pertaining to information only he would know. The deadline for this was at the end of the week, and I emailed him on Monday to allow him a decent amount of time to respond. Tuesday went by, Wednesday, Thursday, and I heard nothing. I sent follow-up emails—but still nothing.

I even stopped by his office twice during the week, hoping that in-person visits would quickly break loose the information I needed. Both times he told me he was busy but that he would get back to me as soon as he could. He didn't.

Friday came, and I had to submit what I had, which was not complete without this piece of information. I felt as though my manager had thrown me under the bus, and it jeopardized my job and reputation.

Their impact. Having the Non-Responder in an office can lead to the distress of coworkers, and frustration over not getting answers or the help they need in a timely fashion. This can be detrimental to the work that is produced from the team if questions are not being answered. This will cause stress and frustration for those working with this person. Other coworkers can feel self-conscious, and they can feel as though the Non-Responder is actively avoiding their questions out of annoyance or dislike.

This has a ripple effect as well. If the person working directly with the Non-Responder is not getting answers or a clear direction for their project, it may cause incomplete or late assignments. This will create negative side effects for the entire company.

CHARACTERISTICS.

- Typically does not care about the needs of their coworkers
- May often seem angry or bitter
- Can be standoffish

- Tends to be absent
- Usually oblivious to their actions
- Can be a distracted person

SURVEY.

1. Are you or a coworker bad at responding to people in a timely manner?

2. Do you or a coworker frequently forget to respond?

3. Do you or a coworker not care about responding to people?

4. Are you or a coworker non-responsive out of spite?

5. Are you or a coworker an easily distracted person?

If you answered "Yes" to two or more of these questions, you or your coworker are on the spectrum of being the Non-Responder.

The Chatter

Who are they? These people are the types that will stop by your desk whenever they desire, and they will talk non-stop. True to their name, the Chatter likes to chat about anything and everything—they can have a full-on conversation with the wall if there are no humans around to talk to. No matter how many hints you drop about how busy you are, they will not seem to get it.

It's great to have an office with people who like to communicate openly and frequently with one another about work-related topics, but the Chatter takes it one step too far. They don't care what they're talking about, and chances are it won't be about anything work related (unless the Chatter happens to also be the Gossiper). Whether you are being talked to by the Chatter or you're hearing the Chatter talking in the background, both of these scenarios make a negative impact in the office. Every coworker will most likely fall victim to the Chatter's way at some point or another.

Case study. On my first day at my current job, I was extremely nervous. It was the typical first-day anxiety of not having friends, not being right for the position, messing up, and the list goes on. When I got acquainted at my new job that day, one of my coworkers came by to introduce herself. Lindsay seemed nice, and genuinely interested in my life. We chatted for a bit, and my boss came over to hand me some paperwork, and she walked back to her desk. I was happy that someone had opened up to me—at least I'd made one friend so far.

Throughout the week, Lindsay would make frequent stops at my desk to check in and talk about her personal life or work. To be honest, this was a nice mental break and I enjoyed her presence. It wasn't until a few weeks into the job that I started to become very busy with my first assignment. This was the first time I could prove my skills to my team. I was tirelessly working on this, but Lindsay seemed to consistently get in the way. I would be deep in concentration, and then she'd walk up and start talking about politics, her cat, or what she did over the weekend. I didn't want to be rude and ask her to leave, so I just sat there, barely listening.

It became quite frustrating because her chatting broke my concentration and impacted my productivity and work ethic. It got to the point where I finally worked up the nerve to tell her that I was on a tight deadline, and really needed to concentrate on my own work. She seemed to understand, and she walked away.

I then began to realize that Lindsay's chatting throughout the office became annoying background noise that took away from my concentration as well. I would find myself drifting off, distracted by her pointless conversations. But she continued to talk the ears off of other coworkers, which was just as distracting as her talking to me. Luckily, I got my assignment in on time, but this is something I struggled to stand my ground with.

Their impact. Having the Chatter in your office can lead to frustration and a lack of productivity when this coworker forces you out of "work mode" to listen to whatever it is they have to talk about for what feels like hours. It can be difficult for a coworker to tell the Chatter to stop talking, for fear of being rude, which leads to pent-up anger and frustration. With constant chatter in the office, it's difficult to maintain high productivity levels and complete concentration on work. In worst-case scenarios, the Chatter can lead to lower-quality work and missed deadlines, which can ultimately hurt a company.

CHARACTERISTICS.

- Friendly and social
- Talks more than anyone else in the room
- Enjoys being the center of attention
- Never runs out of things to talk about
- Lacks self-awareness—does not realize their harm
- Is distracted from their own work
- Bad work ethic

SURVEY.

1. Do you or a coworker talk more than others at the office?

2. Do you or a coworker enjoy being the center of attention?

3. Are you or a coworker distracted at work?

4. Do you or a coworker not have a problem with going up to people who are in the middle of working to chat about non-work-related topics?

5. Has anyone ever had to tell you or a coworker to stop talking?

If you answered "Yes" to two or more of these questions, you or your coworker are on the spectrum of being the Chatter.

The Absent One

Who are they? This is the type of person who is typically the last to get to work, and the first to leave. The Absent One is usually distracted at work with things like social media or miscellaneous personal matters. Sometimes these are people who slack at their job and rely on others to pick up their extra work. They don't seem to care about their job or the people they work with. They don't try to bond with the team or do anything that is considered "extra."

Usually, the Absent One is someone who is not passionate or interested in their work and would rather be elsewhere. Sometimes, they use their day to work on their own personal side projects that do not relate to their job whatsoever. These are people who are constantly distracted, and they are never 100 percent mentally present at work.

Case study. My friend Jeff was one of my really great friends in the office. We both started around the same time, and we quickly became really close. About eight months into our job, I noticed a change in him. He interacted less with all of us, the quality of his work decreased, and overall, he just didn't seem present. I would occasionally stop by his desk to say "Hi," and I would notice him working on something that didn't relate to what we were doing at all.

This happened a few times, and I decided to confront him about it since we were friends. He said not to tell anyone, but he was working on his own startup company, and he was hoping to leave this job once it became successful. I was happy for him that he was following his dreams with the startup, but it didn't feel right that he was working on his personal project while being paid to be at work. It didn't seem fair to the rest of us on the team, especially since we've had to pick up some of the extra work that Jeff ended up not doing.

This experience left me feeling disheartened and frustrated. It also made me feel like our job had less value since Jeff wasn't prioritizing it. I noticed some of his ways rubbing off on me. I started to become more distracted at work, scrolling on Facebook and shopping on Amazon. At a certain point, I couldn't help but feel guilty that a company was paying me for a job that I was neglecting. I decided to not follow in Jeff's footsteps, and to help my team and company succeed by giving my job 100 percent of my effort while I was at work.

Their impact. The Absent One may not seem like they have an impact on the office, but they really do. When one person starts doing non-work-related things in the office, this gives the go-ahead for others to follow suit. This can cause a domino effect that creates a huge issue among the team. The Absent One in the office will tend to slack off on work, leaving the rest of the team with the burden of carrying their coworker's weight.

It also becomes very disheartening when a team member doesn't seem to care about the well-being of their coworkers and company. People may also become frustrated that this person is getting paid to do nothing, while others may be working more, yet they are making the same amount of income—or even less. It reinforces a careless, distracted, absent mindset for the office. This can get out of hand, and it can become difficult for managers and bosses to control.

CHARACTERISTICS.

- Distracted with non-work-related things
- Usually leaves the office early, and gets to the office late
- Doesn't partake in any extracurricular office events
- During office hours, emphasizes personal priorities over work priorities
- Lacks self-awareness of the negative impact they have on a team
- Is not usually mentally present at the office

SURVEY.

1. Do you or a coworker usually do non-work-related things throughout the day?
2. Are you or a coworker distracted at work?
3. Do you or a coworker typically not take part in non-mandatory office events?
4. Do you or a coworker usually leave the office early, and/or get to the office late?
5. When at the office, is your job not a priority for you or a coworker?

If you answered "Yes" to two or more of these questions, you or your coworker are on the spectrum of being the Absent One.

PART II

EIGHT STRATEGIES FOR DEALING WITH JERKS AT WORK

Dream big, start small, but most of all, start.

—SIMON SINEK

Once you've identified the toxic people in your workplace (perhaps including yourself), you'll need to take action to neutralize the negative impact they have on you, your coworkers, and customers and other stakeholders. In this Part, I provide you with eight proven, research-based strategies for countering and neutralizing jerks at work. The advice in these chapters applies whether you're an employee or a manager—providing specific recommendations that you can put to work right now. Topics include:

- Disconnecting from emotions
- Refusing to play their game
- Learning how to neutralize conflict
- Challenging bad behavior
- Not sweating the small stuff
- Learning by negative examples
- Not being a jerk yourself
- Hiring slow, firing fast

3

TAKE A BIG STEP BACK

*If you don't like something, change it. If you
can't change it, change your attitude.*

—MAYA ANGELOU

N ow that we've explored all of the different types of jerks
at work you most likely have encountered during the
course of your career and life—and have yet to encounter—
let's take a big step back. You may feel overwhelmed knowing that you're working with one or more toxic people, but
don't be too concerned at this point. In this chapter, we'll
explore ways to help you understand and (believe it or not)
successfully work with these people.

When you're working one on one every day with these
jerks at work, one of the first reactions you may have is to let
your emotions get the best of you. These people will push
your buttons, they'll play with your emotions, and it's easy

to let them get the best of you. We often let our emotions get in the way of how we view things rationally. This leads to a multitude of issues in the workplace such as reduced productivity, hampered happiness, lowered confidence, and pervasive discomfort.

When you react to whatever game it is that the jerk is playing, you're giving that person some measure of control over you because they know what to do to get you to react in a way that gets them what they want. It's those specific buttons that they push that get them excited—as you start to feel bad, they start to feel good. In order to feel energized and content, they feed off of your emotions.

This is the type of workplace toxicity that we need to avoid and remove from our lives. But, in order to do this, we first need to take a big step back. To be specific, take the 50,000-foot view of your situation. By doing this, you will have a bird's-eye perspective of what's really going on between you and the jerk. You will have the ability to rationally assess the situation and understand who this person is and why they're doing what they're doing.

Is it because of their own insecurities? Is it because they are competitive? Is it because they are only looking to leverage their career by putting everyone else down? Ask questions and analyze the situation.

It's important to think long and hard about the person who is causing you and your coworkers so much trouble. Taking a step back will allow you to do this, and it will also allow you to understand the situation from a different perspective. When you're up close and personal with a jerk at work, it's easy to let your emotions get the best of you. Take a big step back and look at the person or situation from a more distant perspective—the 50,000-foot view.

There are five steps you need to take in order to achieve this. We will go through each one so that you can begin to neutralize the toxicity that is a part of your workplace. Each step is important to the process, and the outcomes will be better the more work you put in.

1. REFUSE TO GET CAUGHT UP IN THE EMOTION

It's no big secret that we human beings have feelings—we're creatures of emotion. While there's nothing we can do about that fact, being at the whim of our emotions has its positives and its negatives. We all know about the flight-or-fight response—the internal cascade of hormones and other powerful chemicals that prepare us to confront a threat. If we're out on a hike and encounter a hungry grizzly bear, then this response can be very handy—it can in fact save our life. However, when we're in an office situation, this chemical cascade can get in the way of our rational thought processes.

Our body's reaction to the fight-or-flight response fires up in very interesting ways. We get that rush of adrenaline and our stomach feels like it's turning upside down, we begin to sweat, our cheeks flush, and some of us even develop a nervous tick—a bouncing knee, a twitchy foot, nail biting, blinking too rapidly, or speaking too quickly. This fight-or-flight reaction is perfectly normal, but the emotions that are unleashed may cause us to overreact to that jerk who is pushing our buttons.

When that office jerk pushes one of our buttons, we are suddenly flooded with emotions that we have trouble controlling. We aren't able to think straight or react in a way that is beneficial to us. Instead, we provide the exact reaction that the toxic person is hoping to get out of us. With this success in hand, they'll continue to push that button—causing another emotional reaction—or they'll probe until they find a completely different button to push. It's a cycle that goes on and on until we decide to make a change within ourselves—taking a big step back and refusing to get caught up in the emotion.

When someone is being a jerk at work, take a look at your own emotional reaction. Think back on times that you have reacted to jerks you've worked with:

- *What were you doing?*

- *What was your reaction?*

- *How were you feeling?*

- *Were you defensive?*

- *Did you feel emotional?*

- *Were you upset?*

- *Was this emotion getting in the way of your thinking about a positive course of action? Or was it just getting you more wound up and more drawn into the toxicity that this person was releasing in the workplace?*

Asking questions such as these—and paying attention to your responses—are important steps to understanding and eliminating your emotional reaction and enhancing your rational reaction.

Case study. At my previous job, I had a super-mean coworker named Molly. At the end of each quarter, every member on the team would give a small presentation about their achievements—essentially a personal end-of-quarter review. I remember being particularly excited about mine because for the first time ever, I was proud about what I had accomplished as a first-time team leader.

After my presentation, my boss congratulated me on my achievements, and said she looked forward to my work next quarter. This gave me the boost of confidence I needed at that point in my career. When our meeting ended, I was walking to the restroom when Molly stopped me. I remember her words were like daggers: "Your work may be decent but just know you will never be the leader of any company or team. You're meant to be a subordinate. You have no natural leadership qualities at all, so don't try to pretend like you do. We all know you would never be fit."

Molly's words took me completely off guard, my heart stopped, and I felt that tight feeling in my chest. I had no idea what to say, so I walked straight to the restroom and started crying. It was my impulse reaction; I couldn't help it. My fight-or-flight response decided on flight. There was no way I wanted to risk Molly or my other coworkers seeing me cry, so I had to go to the restroom as quickly as I could. Those words hit me hard.

I decided to take a few breaths, and to take a step back. I had to force my mind out of my dark thoughts. I asked myself important personal questions about how and why I reacted the way I did. I checked in with myself to make sure that what Molly said to me actually was really hurtful, and it wasn't just me getting worked up for no reason. By asking myself these questions, I grew frustrated that my initial reaction was to flee the scenario, and that it wasn't to just stand my ground with her. I continued to evaluate the situation, my reaction, and my thoughts. I continued to take that step back from my emotions the rest of the day at work.

2. TAKE A LOOK FROM THE OUTSIDE IN

The next step is to take a look at the behavior that the office jerk is engaging in. Try to step out of your situation for a moment and look at the behavior from someone else's perspective—a coworker, a customer, your boss.

If you put yourself in a fellow coworker's mind, or even your boss's mind, what do you think their perspective would be? *What would they think? How would they classify this behavior? Would they think it's the same? Would they have the same reaction as you? Why or why not?* Try to get an outside perspective in order to garner a better understanding of the issue at hand, and how you are reacting to it.

To refresh your memory, look back at Chapter 2, A Field Guide to the Sixteen Most Common Jerks at Work. Take a look at those different kinds of jerks and try to figure out which kind of jerk this person is. Keep in mind that they may not embody every single characteristic on the list. Since each person is on a spectrum, people will have varying degrees of similarities to each toxic personality. If the person seems to relate to a specific personality the most, they are probably that type of person. Also, keep in mind that this person may be a hybrid. For example, they may be both the Intimidator and the Gossiper.

While going through the list, write down the specific office jerks that relate to the person, along with their corresponding attributes in order to more thoroughly understand who they are. Make sure to get out of your own personal, biased perspective while doing this. Think from the perspective of someone in your office who is more distant from the issue or person and not caught up in the emotion since they would be looking at this more objectively than maybe you are.

Case study. After spending the rest of my workday trying to distance myself from my emotions, I decided to think a bit more deeply about this Molly situation. If I didn't do this, I knew that Molly's words would be something very emotionally damaging to me. It could hurt the way I went about my work, and it could even hurt my career aspirations due to the low self-esteem I felt as a result of Molly's attack.

I decided to take a few more steps back and assess this from my coworkers' and my boss's perspective. *What would my boss or coworker think if they saw this interaction I had with Molly? If they were in my shoes, what would they think? How would they react?*

After answering these questions, I realized that what Molly said was objectively mean. I can't imagine anyone thinking that her words were pleasant. Based on my boss's confidence and control, her reaction would have been much different than mine—hers would be more fight, less flight. My other coworkers, however, may have had a more similar reaction to mine. We were all still early on in our careers, trying to find our places within our industry. I considered the list of the most common jerks at work and jotted down the names and characteristics that Molly seemed to embody the most based on my experiences with her.

Below are the types of jerks I decided on:

The Intimidator: Standoffish, will threaten for personal gain, manipulative, abrasive, well spoken, elitist.

The Envier: Shows competitive impulses, angry or hostile towards people they're envious of, feels they're better than the person they're envious of, status and clout is important to this person.

The Malicious One: Standoffish, feels superior, aggressive, lacks morality and kindness, isn't afraid to say what they're thinking, straight-up mean, self-absorbed.

The Pessimist: Always negative, nothing is ever perfect or good enough, asserts their cynical viewpoint on others.

Writing these out made me feel better. I realized that my thoughts and feelings about Molly were not all just in my head. Maybe she was one or a few of these office jerks. It also made me hopeful that I could move past this and learn how I could continue to coexist with her in the same office space.

3. FIGURE OUT WHAT BUTTONS THE JERK IS PUSHING

We all have buttons that people will try to push at some point or another. It's called being human. Some buttons cause sad reactions, while other buttons cause anger or embarrassment—they can really cause just about any emotion.

Toxic people are experts at finding these buttons, which causes us to express the specific emotions that are triggered. Earlier on in my career, when I was working my second big job out of college, I had a coworker who was very envious of me coming in at a pretty young age and doing the job that she was assigned to do. We were both contract negotiators, and she thought that she was the top-dog contract nego-tiator. She was very upset that I had been brought in, and her reaction to this was to push my buttons—and she was pretty successful at it.

Sometimes she figured out what would get a reaction from me, and I would get upset. I was young and didn't have any guidance at this point in time to understand how I could work with individuals like her. If I could, I would tell my younger self to take a look at those buttons that you have and assess what it is that this jerk is pushing. Try to get a feel for what it is. This may take time to assess deeply, but it's extremely important that you're able to take this time.

If the person is making you feel lesser than them and inadequate for the job, maybe that button they're pressing is a specific insecurity you have deep down inside. Once you pinpoint this, you will be able to understand these deep-rooted issues that we all have within ourselves and are manifested into "buttons." These can be personal insecurities, self-confidence issues, anger issues, competitive issues—just about anything.

Once you step outside of yourself, take a big step back, and look at your emotional reactions, you can start to work backward and see what that person did to make you react the way that you did. *What did the person say? What did the person do? How did they get me to react?* And once you've identified the buttons that this person is pushing, then you can neutralize your reactions, and prevent them in the future. Getting to know the button is the first step. Don't be afraid to do a deep dive into your mind and emotions in order to understand what your buttons are, and why they exist.

Case Study. After I thought more thoroughly about the type of office jerk Molly could be, I took a few steps even further back and turned the attention on myself. I needed to understand why I reacted the way I did, and what the in-depth explanation was for my hurt feelings. Why couldn't I just brush off her words? Or why couldn't I have just stood up for myself? It took me a while, but taking a step back from my emotions helped me narrow in on what the source of my reaction was.

I realized that Molly's words directly linked to my insecurities of never being in a leadership position but always quietly wanting to be. I was never one to be seen in leadership roles throughout my entire life, and it never seemed like I would ever be a leader in any shape or form. At work, I had slowly been moving toward more leadership positions and I finally felt somewhat confident in my ability. My boss had even made me the lead on one of our biggest projects of that past quarter.

The confidence in my ability of being a leader was amplified after my successful presentation, and when Molly said those hateful words during the peak of my pride, it hurt. She cut down all of the confidence I had accumulated over a period of time, and she wiped it out of me. After I found out that this leadership insecurity was the button for me, I realized that this was something I could overcome. Just because Molly knew how to manipulate my emotions that one time didn't mean I would let her continue.

4. ASK OTHERS WHAT THEY THINK

What do other people think? Does this jerk see the same things that you're seeing? Get that outside perspective of someone else—your coworkers, your boss, perhaps even your customers. What kinds of behavior do they see this person engaging in? Do they seem to agree with your own experience? Do they also see this person as a jerk? Are their buttons being pushed by this person as well?

If there is one or more who have been negatively impacted by this person, what can you do together in order to help this situation? Are you able to band together with others who are also victims of the jerk's ways? If so, pull together your information and maybe confront this person or your boss, and deal with the problem head on. Having allies in the office who can help you deal with an office jerk can be extremely helpful and supportive.

But in order to have this support, you have to ask questions. It can be intimidating, or even embarrassing, to open up to coworkers about what someone has done to make you feel the way you do. However, it is important to do this in order to get an outside perspective. You also may be able to find a group of people who have been feeling the same way about a specific person but may be too afraid to address it. When you take a step back and really look at this jerk, often the feedback of others can be very helpful in assessing exactly what kind of behavior they're engaging in, and what you can do about it.

Case study. The next day at work, I decided to ask a few of my coworkers about their experiences with Molly. It was important that I got an outside perspective so that I wasn't all in my head about this situation. I was curious whether or not they had had any experiences with her in the past. I never thought of Molly as the most pleasant person, but I wasn't sure if she had ever been blatantly mean to other people in our office like she had been to me.

The first person I approached was my coworker, Eli, who had the same job position as me, but had been working at the company for longer. He confided in me that someone had quit this job because of an issue she had with Molly, and that Molly has created a string of issues throughout the time she had been there. This was reassuring to me that I wasn't overreacting or taking things too harshly. I told Eli what had happened to me, and he said not to take it personally—"It's just what she does when she feels like she's being threatened."

This was unsettling, but it made sense if she reacted the way she did based on the success of my presentation that day. I then decided to speak to another one of my coworkers, Taylor, who was in a different job position than I was, but also on our team. She told me that when she was new to the office, Molly commented on her physical appearance, which was hard for Taylor to overcome. It left her with low self-esteem for the months following. It wasn't until she saw Molly say mean things to other people that she realized that Molly was the one with the issues—not her. I continued to speak to a few others throughout the day who said similar things as Eli and Taylor had. They all offered helpful advice on how to deal with Molly, and it made me feel much better about the whole situation.

5. FIGURE OUT WHAT KIND OF JERK YOU'RE DEALING WITH AND ACT ACCORDINGLY

For this step, let's revisit Chapter 2. Apply the model and framework in that chapter to the person who is being toxic to figure out exactly which of those categories of behaviors they're applying. Read through it thoroughly and look back at that list you wrote out in Step 2 about the different types of office jerks you think the person may be.

Now that you have more insight about this person after accomplishing the past few steps, try to hone this list a bit more. Maybe it is that this person is one particular kind of jerk. Maybe they're envious like the coworker I had early on in my career, or maybe they are engaging in multiple behaviors. Figure out exactly what kind of jerk you're dealing with, and then take the advice that is in the field guide for how to deal with them. Take that part and actually put it to action.

Case study. The final step I took in order to settle this issue with Molly was to look over my previous list of potential office jerks she could be. After going through all of the following steps and talking to others in the office about their experiences with Molly, I was able to decipher her ways, and understand who she was. My original list had the Intimidator, the Envier, the Malicious One, and the Pessimist. After going through all of the characteristics with my new knowledge and understanding, I was even more certain about what office jerk she was. She had the most similar characteristics to both The Malicious One and The Envier.

She embodies the Malicious One because of her hurtful words and lack of empathy, along with other traits. The words she said to me were brutally mean—a trait that is quintessentially the Malicious One. She also showed strong signs of the Envier since she would belittle people whenever she felt envious of their successes. Eli's words about her being hostile and mean to those she feels threatened by parallels the Envier's ways.

Having pinpointed the types of office jerks she embodied, I was able to then understand how to deal with her in the office. This helped me immensely as I carried on with moving up in the company. I was able to grow my confidence, and not let Molly faze me. She continued to say things here and there, but I learned to take her words with a grain of salt. This of course wasn't easy, but it was worth the effort for my overall success and happiness.

One of the first things you should do while you're attempting to deal with a toxic person at work is to take a huge step back. Step out of your emotions, step out of your own reaction from the situation at hand. Now sever ties and divorce yourself from that reaction, take a sober and objective look into the scenario. It is not productive to linger on our reaction—move on from it and look at it from a different perspective other than your own. Look at what the behavior is that the person is engaging in, how it's affecting you, what your own reaction is. Then, do something about it.

FOUR WAYS TO REGULATE YOUR EMOTIONS WHEN SOMEONE IS PUSHING YOUR BUTTONS

We all face many difficult situations at work—angry customers and clients, incorrect orders, and stressful office policies or dynamics. However, one of the most difficult situations we face is having to deal with a jerk at work. Even though it isn't possible to always escape these tense moments, it is always possible to control your emotions during difficult times.

Being emotionally aware is a good thing and can even enhance your career. But when we allow emotions to take over a situation, we can face tensed muscles, rising blood pressure, anger, withdrawal, and more. Here are four ways to regulate your feelings so you can effectively manage your actions.

1. **Don't forget to breathe.** In moments filled with tension, be mindful of the air passing into and out of your lungs. You can also count your breaths—experts recommend inhaling and exhaling for a count of six breath counts, and then repeating until you are calmer. Focusing on your breath keeps you centered and takes away attention from the physical signs of panic you may be experiencing.

2. **Practice saying a mantra.** Amy Jen Su, managing partner of Paravis Partners and coauthor of *Own the Room*, recommends creating a mantra that you can repeat to yourself. Doing so will help you stay calm. Some example mantras include: "This will pass," "This is about the business," or "Go to neutral."

3. **Move your attention.** Facing a toxic person? Did someone say something critical about you? Work to concentrate less on the most stressful aspects of the situation, and instead focus on the bright side. What progress have you made in this situation? What value are you contributing to finding a solution? When you redirect attention from the negative to the positive, intense emotional reactions are reduced, making way for greater clarity on resolving issues.

4. **Label what is happening.** Fully acknowledge emotional reactions during a stressful period. This means labeling your feelings as you are experiencing them—"I can feel the anger coming" is an example. You can also work to label how another person is feeling as

well. If a coworker goes on a heated rant, rather than reacting with your own anger (which will only escalate the situation), try instead to go beyond the surface of what you see. Perhaps your coworker is acting this way because they are worried about meeting a sales quota, or maybe they are having problems at home.

How we handle our emotions in stressful business situations can make or break professional relationships. However, if you improve your emotional regulation skills, you can make it through any time of emotional turbulence.

4

REFUSE TO PLAY THEIR GAME

*It's not so important who starts
the game but who finishes it.*

—JOHN WOODEN

Jerks love it when you play their game—it ensures that whatever it is they're doing will continue on and on. However, you have the power to do something different. You can choose to refuse to play that toxic person's game. By refusing to play their game, you'll cut off the oxygen that feeds the fire of a jerk's negative behavior.

In any kind of toxic situation, it really does take two to tango. There has to be a toxic person in the workplace and there has to be a victim—the person who is the recipient of the toxic abuse. If you react or engage in the toxic person's ways, they can be as much of a jerk as they desire. If you don't react or engage and get emotionally caught up in their game, however, then they will be sorely disappointed in the lack of reaction and move on to the next victim. Or maybe they'll eventually just stop their behavior completely if everyone refuses to react.

In most organizations, there is always someone the jerk at work can get a rise out of and those whose buttons they can push. The jerk will continue with their games since pushing buttons and getting the reactions that they crave from others gives them satisfaction. It seems like there is always someone to play the game with them, but that doesn't mean that *you* have to be that person. You don't have to be the victim and you don't have to play these jerks' games.

Now is the time to stand up for yourself and to change the energy and the outcomes. You can refuse and take a stance by not engaging or reacting and refusing to be part of the game the toxic person is playing.

In this chapter, we will explore five strategies for fending off the jerk at work who has a knack for playing with your emotions. These steps will go through how you can refrain from playing their game—no matter how difficult it may seem.

1. FIGURE OUT WHAT GAME THE JERK IS PLAYING

There are all sorts of games that toxic people play at work in order to get an emotional reaction from people. It could be something as simple as saying that they saw the work you did but weren't impressed. They might talk behind your back to others. Or they might get a thrill out of trying to make you look bad in front of your boss during weekly staff meetings. Whatever the case, jerks at work try to trigger your emotions and get a reaction out of you by pushing your buttons. These button pushes come in the form of toxic attacks—some small, others large—meant to create an emotional reaction in you.

Every jerk has something that motivates them to do what they do. Some toxic people enjoy watching their coworkers suffer, while others try to make their coworkers look bad so they look better in comparison. Some are insecure and others are simply hurtful and mean. They achieve their desired results using an assortment of techniques, which we explored in Chapter 2. Make sure to continue to look back at this field guide throughout this step to help with your analysis.

To figure out what is motivating the jerk at work to do what he or she does, take a step back—a 50,000-foot view. This will help you to avoid getting caught up in the emotion generated by the situation, and you will be able to take the next step in figuring out what game the jerk is playing and what reaction they're trying to get out of you. By taking a step back, you're able to analyze the behavior of this person from a completely different and better perspective. This enables you to separate your emotions from your rational mind—which is very important while analyzing what this jerk wants from you. Try to figure out what emotions this person is trying to get from your reaction and address it.

Case study. Last year, I found myself in a dilemma at work. My coworker Jacob and I were assigned to work on a project together. At our first meeting, we assigned roles and tasks that each of us would do. We both agreed to it, and we decided to start working independently on our tasks. Everything was going well at first, but it wasn't until our deadline creeped up on us that things started to get weird.

I had almost finished everything that I was assigned to do, but it didn't seem like Jacob had completed anywhere near the amount of work he should have accomplished by that point in time. At our check-in meeting, he didn't have any plans on finishing it either. He started off his updates by saying to me, "You are going to finish this work for both of us or else I'll have to talk to our boss about what a deadbeat employee you are. I've been here for many years, so don't even bother getting out of this unless you want to be fired."

When he said this, I had no idea how to react—I was dumbfounded. I was scared, and afraid. And I was caught completely off guard. I didn't want Jacob to tell our boss that I was a "deadbeat employee." Jacob had been at the company for longer and was a bit more senior than I was. I couldn't risk him telling this to our boss.

I agreed to Jacob's demands and ended up doing the rest of the assignment for the two of us. Caving to Jacob's threat was extremely frustrating to me, but at the time I felt I had no choice.

Afterwards, I decided to take a step back and assess this situation—far away and disconnected from my immediate emotions. I thought back to the experience and asked myself some very pointed questions, including, *Why did he feel the need to do this? What were his motives? Why did I feel that I had to cave to his demands?* I also tried to get a better idea about exactly what kind of person I was dealing with. I came to the conclusion that he was using intimidation in order to get something out of me. These intimidation tactics are easy to cave to—especially when the intimidator is more senior. He wanted me to feel afraid and insecure in my position, which would force me to do whatever he said. And I have to admit, he succeeded in doing just that.

2. UNDERSTAND HOW THE JERK IS MANIPULATING YOU

So, once you have figured out what game the jerk is playing, look at how they're using the game for their benefit and exactly how they're playing their toxic game with you. Every jerk has a motivation that determines when and what kinds of games they play with others, and who will be the next victim. To resolve the issue, it's your job to figure out what their motive is and then try to diffuse it. You can best accomplish this by taking a step back so that you can more easily focus on their actions and words rather than your own perspective of the situation.

Ask yourself questions like:

- *Are they trying to manipulate me?*

- *What kind of actions or words are they using?*

- *Are they telling me that I should not do something because they are trying to intimidate me or make me feel guilty?*

- *What exactly are they doing and why are they doing it?*

- *What behavior are they engaging in?*

- *What exactly are they doing to try to make me react and emotionally engage?*

Whatever behavior they're engaging in is their way of manipulating you. There are many different behaviors, so it's important to pay close attention and consult with the field guide in Chapter 2. It will give you a better understanding of how and why the jerk is manipulating you.

Case study. The next step I took to more thoroughly analyze this situation was to understand what game Jacob was playing. He clearly had a reason for doing what he was doing—and it wasn't just to get me to do his work for him. From what I knew about him, he didn't appear to be a slacker, so I assumed his motives must have been elsewhere. When I went back to consider the different types of jerks at work in Step 1, I realized his ways most aligned with the Intimidator. He was trying to intimidate me to do his work, but he also wanted to blatantly cast his superiority and power over me.

In this step, I wanted to take a deeper look into his actions and characteristics that align with the Intimidator's ways. The characteristics of the Intimidator that lined up the most with Jacob were: *Will threaten and/or humiliate for their personal gain; manipulative, narcissistic tendencies; abrasive; portrays himself in a confident, elitist manner; and well spoken.* He wanted me to feel intimidated by the dominance and power that he had over me—and he succeeded at that.

When I think more about our experience working together on this project, I treated him as an equal, as I assumed we all should treat one another in our office. I never gave him special treatment—after all, he wasn't my boss. He may have felt like he didn't have any authority or power over me because of the way I was working with him. Maybe he is the kind of person who likes when people fear him, or when people will go above and beyond to please him. I definitely didn't do that. And in order for him to thrust this authority over me, he chose to use the method of intimidation to manipulate me into doing whatever he wanted.

3. REMOVE THE BUTTONS THEY KEEP PUSHING

When someone who is a jerk at work pushes someone else's buttons, they know they will have a good chance of getting the reaction they want from whoever falls victim. They are really adept at finding those buttons—they know that we all have buttons that can be pressed, every single one of us.

The toxic people in our work lives are experts at figuring out which buttons to push and when to push them. We all have vulnerabilities that we normally tend to hide, but the jerks at work can see right through us.

In this next step, instead of focusing on the jerk, focus on *yourself*. Do some self-reflection and look deep into yourself. Try to figure out what buttons you have, and then do everything you can possibly do to remove them. I know this is easier said than done, but with patience, it is definitely possible.

Let's say a toxic person is pushing your guilt button—he or she is trying to make you feel guilty. Generally, they've been successful, and they've found that they can get the reaction they're hoping for. You most likely reacted the way they wanted you to, which is why they know that pressing your button will work. But if you remove the button by not reacting, it will leave that person confused that they couldn't press your button and attain the reaction they were hoping for. By not reacting, you are effectively removing this button.

Thus, when someone pushes your button, don't react. If you change your mindset about the meaning and worth of the words or actions that these jerks exhibit, this may help you remove the button they keep pushing. Once you have successfully removed that button, you have also removed the leverage that that toxic person had over you.

Case study. After fixating on Jacob so much, I needed to look deep within myself. Why did I cave to his desires and actually do his work for him? At the time I knew this was wrong, but I did it anyway. When I think about it, I doubt my boss would've condoned my doing Jacob's work on top of my own. And if he had known that Jacob was essentially blackmailing me, then I'm sure Jacob would have gotten in big trouble.

As I thought about my reaction, I did some deep digging into how I see myself in the workplace, as well as how others may view me. I realized that I have always thought of myself as a subordinate. Having only been at the company for a year, and being relatively young compared to the rest of the team, I always felt the need to listen to everyone else and to never assert my thoughts or opinions. This was in fact an insecurity of mine—I always felt lesser than others, and I never felt that my opinions were worthy compared to the rest in my office.

Jacob clearly saw this and chose to manipulate one of my weakest points. This was my button. Now, I had to eliminate this button, which was much harder than I anticipated. It took me awhile to practice being assertive, and not care about the potential of others thinking my ideas were worthless or dumb. Once I did this, I felt more confident and secure in my position as an important employee to our company. I also had to mentally prepare myself to never cave to Jacob's ways again—or to anyone who tried to intimidate me for that matter. I finally reached the point that if a coworker intimidated me, I would refuse to fall victim to their ways. This felt relieving to know that I was able to eliminate this button that had caused issues throughout my career.

4. GET THAT JERK OUT OF YOUR LIFE

While you may still have to work with this toxic person— especially if they are your boss or on your team—you should try to get them out of your life as much as you possibly can. If the jerk is a coworker, try to get assigned to a different project or a different team. Ask your boss for help and support in dealing with this toxic person. Avoid them when possible, or simply refuse to engage when they try to bait you into a toxic situation.

If the jerk is your boss, then you've got an even bigger problem. Ideally, you should try to get this person out of your life without actually going as far as quitting your job. First, try to work through the issues with your boss, but if that doesn't work, then see if you can be assigned to a different work unit, office, or department. And if you've tried all of these methods but *none* of them work, then consider looking for a new job. Sometimes there are jerks that may just end up being more detrimental to our mental well-being and career, and they are just not worth the effort. These are only extreme cases, however.

Case study. After my experience with Jacob, any respect or desire to work with him ever again was gone. He was no longer someone I would be able to respect in any personal or professional way. I did my best to avoid him at work, which was successful—I rarely crossed paths with him any-way, so this was easy for me to do.

One thing that I was worried about, however, was get-ting assigned to work with him again, and I was certain it was just a matter of time. Every time our boss would partner us with a coworker for an assignment, I would get major anxiety. I could hear my heart thumping until my name was called along with someone other than Jacob. It wasn't until months after my situation with Jacob that we got assigned to work with each other yet again. I was inter-nally stressing myself out. *Should I just get a grip and work with him? Or should I take a stance and confide in my boss?* Both were risky.

I ultimately decided to speak with my boss about the previous experience I had with Jacob, and our discussion went surprisingly well—he even said that he wished that I had told him earlier. My boss ended up assigning me to a different partner so that I didn't have to feel uncomfort-able working with Jacob. He also said that he would never partner us together again and that he would deal with Jacob directly to make sure he wasn't creating the same problem with other employees. This was extremely helpful in reducing my anxiety about Jacob and removing him from my life as best as I could.

5. ENLIST THE HELP OF OTHERS

Some of the toxic people that we work with can be very persistent, they can wield a lot of power in the workplace, and they can even be our boss. Despite this, I believe that there is strength in numbers. The idea is to find other coworkers who are also being negatively affected by this toxic person and share your stories with them. Review the steps you have taken in this chapter to deal with the jerk at work, and share what kind of behaviors this toxic person is engaging in. See if others are in the same exact situation as you are, and find out where they're being affected by this jerk at work, and then band together to neutralize this toxic person.

The toxic people in the workplace have fun when they get to lob that ball at you and hit you with it. They're hoping you won't return it, and in most cases, no one ever hits the ball back at them. They feel good and they're rewarded by their own behavior based on your reaction. If you don't play the game, and just return the ball to them—or if you refuse to even be hit by the ball that they're throwing at you— you'll be way ahead of the game. You'll be doing exactly what you should do in order to neutralize the toxic behavior in your workplace.

Case study. Another thing that I decided to do while I was trying to figure out the Jacob situation was to talk with my coworkers. I didn't feel completely comfortable confiding in some coworkers I wasn't so close with, but I talked with quite a few who were varying degrees of juniors and seniors in our office. To my surprise, it appeared that most people I had talked with had had a first or a secondhand experience with Jacob at one time or another.

Many of my more junior coworkers had similar experiences to mine while working with him. He seemed to have used different intimidation tactics to get what he wanted whether it was work related or not. I talked to one person who said that Jacob intimidated her into bringing him coffee every morning, which sounded ridiculous and extremely unprofessional.

All of these stories started to merge together, and I realized that Jacob had inflicted his terrible behavior on many people in the office. My situation with him wasn't an isolated experience. It was shocking to me that my coworkers had all just continued to come to work every day with the looming anxiety of Jacob threatening their careers by way of intimidation.

Something had to be done, so I organized a meeting for those who'd had personal experiences with Jacob, and we spoke about what we could do. I told them how I had confided in our boss about him, and how he had been very receptive and helpful. This made them feel hopeful that there was potential of fixing this bad situation for all of us. We decided to set up a meeting with our boss to express our concerns and experiences with Jacob.

I can't deny that I wasn't a bit afraid this would backfire. I didn't want our boss to think we were trying to do his job for him. To my surprise, our boss said that he'd had consistent issues with Jacob, both firsthand and secondhand, and he would decide on what to do about the situation. He thanked us for being honest with him, and we carried on with our day. When we came to work the next morning, Jacob wasn't at his desk and all of his stuff was gone. Our boss announced to us that Jacob would be switching departments. For the first time ever, I felt like I had a voice within our company that actually mattered. Any insecurity button that I had was completely gone, and it felt great.

As soon as you understand the game that the jerk in your office is playing, you'll be able to understand why you react the way you do. By being reflective about a terrible experience, you can get rid of the buttons that cause pain if pressed too hard by others. These buttons that all of us have are removable—we have to start thinking of them as such. Once we acknowledge our personal vulnerabilities, we can start making progress on how we continue to work with these jerks in the office.

By doing this, you can also start to cause a positive shift for others in your office who have had similar issues as you, but who may not have been proactive about it. By going through all of these steps, you will not just be improving your job experience and your mental health, but also potentially that of others in your office. Be a leader and take these steps to refrain from playing the jerk's games.

You've got power within you—it's time to use it.

5

LEARN HOW TO
NEUTRALIZE CONFLICT

If you can't go around it, over it, or through it,
you had better negotiate with it.

—ASHLEIGH BRILLIANT

I n this chapter, we will learn how to neutralize conflict. Conflict is something that is natural and common in every organization. Any time you have two people in the same space, inevitably there will be some sort of conflict. Generally, people get along—most of us don't want to have trouble or extraneous problems at work that cause unnecessary stress in our lives. This is particularly true in professional work environments where those types of situations can lead to issues with your career and professional relationships.

Conflict can occur at a low level, which can be quali-fied as a minor issue. If someone gets momentarily angry at someone for something, this is considered a minor con-flict and doesn't require any special attention from man-agement. But sometimes, the conflict can be at a high level. This is when people essentially go to war with each other. And when that happens, it is something that really needs to be dealt with—no matter how difficult neutralizing the conflict might be.

Small conflicts are normal, and they will typically eventually pass over—people will forgive one another and carry on with their day. On the other hand, large conflicts that disrupt the work or productivity of an office for an extended period of time will always have to be dealt with. Whether you're an employee or a manager, you shouldn't let conflicts get out of hand. You should always try to resolve them no matter what the situation is, or who it involves.

As an employee, it may feel risky or intimidating to approach your manager or boss about a conflict in the office. However, it is necessary to do so in order to help keep your office and team functioning as it should. As a manager, when conflicts are significant and start causing problems such as with productivity and the engagement of employ-ees in their work, you need to deal with that. It is easy to brush off issues and conflicts within the office, but as a manager or a coworker, you need to do something about it. It is important to be proactive about this, so things don't blow out of proportion and get out of hand.

Catch conflict before it escalates out of control by addressing the problem at the earliest stage when it is more easily resolved. To neutralize conflict so that it doesn't continue to grow, there are five essential steps that you must take. Carefully go through this list and take note. These steps are meant for managers and employees of any level. Everyone is able to and should utilize these steps while addressing and solving conflict within the office.

1. OBSERVE OBJECTIVELY

The first step you must take in order to neutralize the conflict at hand is to take a look at the people who are involved in the conflict and analyze and understand their behavior. When you do this, emotionally detach yourself from the feelings that may be surrounding the conflict itself. This will help you take an objective look at the behavior and what is causing the issue. As we did in the previous chapters, step back and take the 50,000-foot view. This is an integral step to understand the roots of the conflict. If you do not do this step, your emotions and your own personal bias will get in the way of solving the issue.

Once you successfully pull back from your emotions to gain perspective, ask yourself these questions: *Is this issue occurring because someone just doesn't like the other person? Is it because someone feels slighted that they're not being treated the way they should be? Is it because someone is troubled, and they are striking out for some reason?* The whole point of this step is to get to the root of the conflict and to observe it objectively, dispassionately, and unemotionally. Detach from the emotion of the conflict and take a look at the way it gives you the real story instead of something colored by emotion and feelings.

Case study. I have been the manager of the marketing team for our company for about five years now, and I have dealt with the occasional office drama from time to time. It's an inevitable occurrence that I can count on erupting at least a few times a year. About a year ago, I experienced one of the more troubling conflicts I have had to deal with in my career thus far.

There are two people on our team, Chelsea and Ryan, who seemed to start off as close friends and coworkers. Over a period of time, I noticed a strange shift between their dynamic—their working relationship began to fall apart, and as it did, the dynamic of the entire office began to change as well. Before, we were a very close and collaborative team. But at some point, it seemed like the entire office became divided. I felt a growing tension among my coworkers, but I had no idea what the reason was. My only idea was that this issue must have had something to do with Chelsea and Ryan, which was too bad, because I really liked them both on a personal and professional level.

I didn't like how my opinion on the two of them changed, and that I felt uneasy and uncertain about them. I knew if I was feeling this way, I'm sure the rest of the office must have been feeling this way too. For that reason, this was definitely an issue that I needed to address. In order to do that, I began by taking that 50,000-foot perspective so I could remove my own emotions and connection with Ryan and Chelsea. I realized that I was letting my emotions color my perspective of this situation—it was preventing me from actually seeing what was going on.

I asked myself questions that I could answer based on an outsider perspective. What I took away from it was: 1) Chelsea and Ryan were the source of this office tension, 2) Chelsea and Ryan no longer got along, 3) Either Chelsea or Ryan caused this conflict with the other—someone said or did something to the other, 4) They have gotten to the point that they refuse to work together and feel uncomfortable around each other—or at least one of them feels this way, and 5) One or both of them must have brought other coworkers into this drama. With this information in hand, I could get a better understanding of what was going on between Chelsea and Ryan and how it was affecting our team.

2. IDENTIFY EMOTIONS

Once you have successfully observed the conflict in its entirety from an objective perspective, you must then identify the exhibited emotions. While going through this next step, continue to maintain that 50,000-foot view in order to analyze the emotions from an unbiased perspective.

When there's a conflict, this means that there is some sort of emotion between two or more people. It could be a group of people who are in conflict, which would involve a lot of types and varying degrees of emotion. People get upset, people get mad, people get angry. These emotions are essentially what conflict is, and inevitably, these emotions boil over. In order to help subdue the emotions at stake, you must try to get to their root. By doing so, this will allow you to attain a better idea of what those emotions might be.

Ask yourself questions like: *Are people feeling hurt? Are people feeling that they're not being listened to? Are people feeling that their ideas are being discarded and not paid attention to? What is the conflict? What are the emotions involved in that conflict?* If you can get an idea of what those emotions are, you are able to answer these questions. It may take time to analyze all of this, but in order for conflict to be resolved, you must put in the effort.

Case study. Now that I was able to observe the issue from a more distant perspective, I needed to identify the emotions that Chelsea, Ryan, and the others in the office had been showing. These were emotions that I may have discredited as a serious thing, and accidentally missed.

Continuing to maintain my distant view of the matter, I delved into the emotions that I had noticed throughout the previous month or so as things began to worsen. People were clearly feeling hurt—I remember seeing Chelsea crying during that time, but of course I didn't want to pry. I'm assuming this is when everything started. She must have been hurt and upset about something, and it might have been something that Ryan said or did. Her being upset caused Ryan to switch locations in the office for some reason—maybe he was trying to get away from her because he felt uncomfortable being around her. Or maybe she had forced him to move?

This caused tension within the office for both of them. Some people were closer with Chelsea and never talked to Ryan, and some were closer to Ryan and never talked to Chelsea. This was a tad confusing to me. If Ryan had said something mean to Chelsea, wouldn't they all be on Chelsea's side? I needed to investigate this further.

3. IDENTIFY UNDERLYING NEEDS

People have needs, and people have wants that they are trying to attain in their own lives. We all have many goals in life that center around our professional work lives, as well as our personal lives. Many times, these needs translate into something that causes unnecessary conflict in the workplace that can negatively impact an entire team.

Try to get an idea of what people's needs are that are motivating them to partake in a specific behavior that is creating conflict. What is motivating them to do what they want to do, or get what they want at work? Once you understand their needs, you will better understand what is getting in the way of them achieving and fulfilling these desires on their own.

It may be possible, for example, that there is another person in the office who is standing in the way of them fulfilling their needs. Maybe there is someone in the office whose need is to be recognized or thanked by their boss for achieving something at work. However, there is another coworker getting in the way of this need. For example, if there is someone who enjoys the spotlight, and steals the work credit of others in the office—they're the one who is getting in the way of a coworker's need being fulfilled because their accolades are being stolen from this coworker.

Once you can identify what the underlying need is, you can then figure out what barriers are getting in the way of someone fulfilling their needs. Taking this step to identify the inherent needs of individuals will really help you understand and resolve the conflict that is causing issues within the office.

Case study. Now, I had to get to the root cause of the issue—I needed to understand why this conflict was happening between the two. Why was Chelsea upset that day? Did Ryan have something to do with it? And why has it caused the team to seemingly take sides, and split in half? I thought back on Chelsea and Ryan, and their parallels and differences that could have caused an issue. They both were around the same age, they both started working on the team at around the same time, and they both had the same position. Right off the bat, I could assume that there must have been a sort of tension about being in the same position that could have potentially caused some sort of competitive feeling.

I went through our meeting agendas from the first few weeks of the previous month, which was around the time I saw Chelsea crying. I realized that I had briefly brought up the potential for one promotion, and that we would be assessing everyone in the upcoming months. This was nothing that I saw as an urgent matter since we weren't looking to fill the the new role for a few more months, but it was meant to be more of an update for those interested. Could this be what caused the conflict?

With two people in the same position at work, trying to reach the next level and fulfill their career goals, this was a possible root cause for the conflict. Maybe Ryan did or said something in order to enhance his potential at getting the promotion, and to knock Chelsea out of the running. Had Chelsea done something to Ryan as well? I needed to know these answers in order to completely understand the conflict that was causing an even bigger conflict among the team as a whole.

4. INVOLVE EMPLOYEES TO UNDERSTAND THE IMPACT OF THEIR BEHAVIOR ON OTHERS

A surprisingly large amount of the time, people don't realize that when they're behaving a certain way, their actions are causing others to feel negative emotions. This behavior can cause hurt, it can cause pain, it can cause their coworkers to be unhappy about them. Even if they are intent on hurting one person, they don't typically realize that their behavior has adverse effects on the team—and the company—as a whole.

Regardless of your position—manager or a coworker—you have the ability to point this out to the person who is causing problems for others. This may sound very intimidating, and a bit scary—particularly if you aren't in a managerial role—but if you don't step up, likely nothing will change.

To go about this, pull the coworker who is causing issues aside privately and point out their behavior in a non-aggressive, calm way. If you use an accusatory tone, or accusatory wording, this could potentially cause that coworker to become defensive and offended. When you are talking to this person, it is important to thoughtfully explain to them what the problem is, and how their behavior has negatively impacted certain people in the office.

For example, if you say that you don't consider someone to be an equal or a partner at work—a co-equal—that person will understandably be upset and sad. It's at the root of the conflict of the two people. Explain how their behavior leads to other negative impacts with other employees, somewhat like a domino effect. Confronting the person about their behavior and their negative impact on other coworkers is never an easy thing to do, but it is an important step to take in order to resolve the conflict.

Case study. In order to address this situation head on, I needed to confront Ryan about the issue I was noticing. Since he was the one who was seemingly exhibiting the bad behavior, he was the one I needed to meet with to discuss how that behavior was hurting our team. I decided to ask Ryan to come to my office for a one-on-one meeting the following day.

When he walked in, he seemed to be dressed fancier than usual, and he was overly nice and complimentary. The Ryan I had known for the past few years did not seem to be the schmoozy type that he was embodying at that moment. Did he think that I was going to give him a promotion right then and there? I sat him down, and I told him I wanted to address something that had seemingly gotten worse and worse by the week.

I expressed to him that I had noticed a growing tension within the office, and it seemed to start around the same time that he switched desk locations. I also explained how I knew that there was something bad going on between him and Chelsea, and I needed him to know that this was causing major issues within the entire team. Whatever he said or did was not only creating conflict with Chelsea, but his coworkers as well.

I could tell he was caught off guard and didn't know what to say. He sunk in his chair a bit and took a deep breath. He apologized and said that he didn't realize that his words would cause so much drama that would seep through the entire office. Without my prompting him, Ryan confessed to me that when I mentioned the promotion at our meeting, he was very excited and suddenly became overly competitive about it. He knew that Chelsea was the only one who was qualified to beat him out for this position, and he wanted to make sure she wasn't standing in his way. He ended up gossiping among the team about things Chelsea had confided in him about— personal things that made her sound bad. He didn't mention exactly what those things were, but they clearly weren't good.

This explained why the team was divided, and that they didn't all take Chelsea's side. I had asked him if any of those things Chelsea had said that he gossiped about had to do with others in the office, and he nodded his head. I explained to him that the drama he caused would be extremely difficult to mend. Gossiping is a toxic behavior that not only impacts the person you're trying to hurt, but it can also hurt others in the office. He seemed to understand, and he was very apologetic about it.

5. ENCOURAGE RESOLUTION

No one wants conflict to persist in the workplace—unless we're the jerks at work who are causing the conflict, we much prefer for it to be resolved. To reemphasize, minor conflict is normal, and it is nothing to really worry about. So, don't stress too much unless it becomes something much larger. When specific conflicts that are clearly bigger and more persistent cause problems at work—and people become distracted, less engaged, and their performance is lowered—that is when you need to deal with the conflict.

In order to deal with the conflict, encourage resolution by bringing all opposing parties together. First, take each of the people aside individually to get their side of the story, privately in your office. Get Person A's story and get Person B's story, and then once you have a good understanding of their perspectives of the conflict at hand, bring them both together to talk it out.

During this time, figure out the specific issues that are seemingly causing the conflict. Once you have addressed the issues with them in a private place, move this meeting out in the open. You can go on a walk, or sit in a public space, and encourage the parties to work through these issues with you. As you explain what their impacts are, make sure to go through the previous steps with them when you're explaining the impacts of their behavior on each other, and others in the office.

Try to work it out with them, step by step. This may take time, and some may be less than excited about this conversation, but it is necessary. Throughout this step, the person who is engaging in the toxic behavior will start to realize the negative impact of their behavior, and then they will work on quitting their engagement in the behavior. At that point, you have successfully neutralized the conflict, and helped save your team a lot of grief and lost productivity.

Case study. It was a huge relief getting Ryan's side of the story. I felt more confident in the potential of resolving this issue and being able to possibly help mend Ryan and Chelsea's broken relationship. It's difficult and can be nearly impossible to work on a team with someone you dislike. I liked both Ryan and Chelsea, and I didn't want them to feel discomfort toward each other. This could cause even more serious issues in the future, making the team as a whole more toxic than it already was.

I ended up sending both of them an email to meet me in my office, but I wanted to briefly meet with each of them separately beforehand. I met with Chelsea first, and told her the situation. I could tell she was extremely uncomfortable, but also calm. She explained to me more in detail about the gossip that Ryan had spread about her. He said things such as she only got the job because her aunt was an executive at our company, and different things she had said about other coworkers behind their backs.

She clarified that she didn't mean everything that she said but sometimes gets worked up in the moment and thought she could vent to Ryan without him spreading it to the entire team. Chelsea also said that the recent team dynamic had made her feel extremely uncomfortable and ostracized once this all started. Many people on the team refused to talk to her or work with her because of this. She also still had no idea why Ryan had done this, which caused her even more pain.

I met with Ryan separately next, and quickly explained to him that I was going to bring them together so that we could solve this issue. He agreed, and he walked into my office and sat next to Chelsea. Now that I knew both sides of their story, we went through the timeline and each event that had happened. Starting from the promotion announcement, to Ryan's gossiping, Chelsea crying, Ryan moving desks, and to current day—a divided office. We came to the conclusion that this was done out of the need to reach that promotion, and to fulfill Ryan's career dream.

Chelsea seemed distressed and angry. I decided to move this conversation outside in public so we could get fresh air and talk through the issues together. It took a while for both Ryan and Chelsea to feel better about each other. Chelsea had been hurt very badly, and Ryan didn't completely understand how terribly his actions had impacted her. He offered an apology and said he would never do that to anyone ever again.

All three of us came to the conclusion that Ryan and Chelsea should meet with our team as a group and discuss the events that took place. Both of them needed to apologize for causing hurt feelings, discomfort, and tension on the team. After our meeting, all of us felt like we could finally move past this issue—Ryan even moved back to his old desk next to Chelsea in order to mend their relationship. These steps were hugely impactful for their relationship, and our entire team's relationships with one another.

Neutralizing conflict is something we all should be able to do. It may seem daunting whether you are a manager or employee, but it is something that is necessary in order to solve the issue. If you are an employee and don't feel like you are in the position to take these steps, address this with your manager. If you're not good at it, this chapter should help guide you in successfully putting out the fire in the office.

HOW TO DEAL WITH HAVING A STRONG PERSONALITY

Have you ever been told that you have a "strong" personality?

If so, it's likely you intimidate others. Perhaps you're domineering in conversations, hard-headed, and unafraid to use your voice. Or, you may find it a challenge to settle for anything less than what you feel you deserve.

Don't feel discouraged if others perceive you as scary—the reality is that having a strong personality can actually yield you a near-endless supply of benefits. If you want to successfully handle having a strong personality, you should accept and embrace the traits and mindset you have, while recognizing and understanding how others may react to you.

If you're a leader with a strong personality, acknowledge your power but make sure you're not always grabbing the reins. Your strength of character will make it feel natural to control every situation, so you must lead in a non-dictatorial fashion. Give others a turn to put forth and advocate for ideas, and practice thoroughly listening to the feedback your peers or subordinates give. A collaborative work environment will be more creative and more enjoyable for the workforce, business, or organization as a whole.

If you're a team member with a strong personality, be careful not to rub your peers the wrong way. There will be many occasions where taking a relaxed and personable approach to working in a team will be more effective. Although competition is your forte as a strong personality, too much aggressive and unnecessary competition between you and other members of your team will ultimately be detrimental to your task or mission. If you're always looking to emerge victorious or most powerful in every setting, you will miss out on the benefits of real and authentic collaboration.

Having a strong personality gives you resilience, focus, and incredible self-belief—you know anything can be accomplished so long as you put your mind to it. A strong personality is a rarity and a gift, and if you appreciate and utilize it properly, you will be brought to new heights.

6

SEE SOMETHING, SAY SOMETHING

We have to stop rewarding bad behavior.

—NATALIE COLE

Whether you're a manager or a frontline employee, don't let bad behavior go unaddressed or unchallenged. When you ignore bad behavior instead of dealing with it, you're just giving the jerk permission to continue to do what they're doing.

In my own experience, one of the biggest mistakes people make when they have a bad situation with a jerk at work is that they just try to ignore it. They try to hide and downplay the issue, and they avoid confronting the person who is engaging in the bad behavior. People tend to downplay issues because they don't want to potentially draw negative attention to themselves, or they don't want to get on someone's bad side. This is a mistake.

When you don't confront the person or address their bad behavior, then the jerk at work will often take advantage of the situation and keep behaving badly. Things will only get worse instead of better. For that reason, instead of ignoring the bad behavior, openly call out the jerk and explain what negative thing they are doing so that this doesn't go ignored and unattended. It may sound intimidating to do this—particularly if you are new to the job or a junior employee—but it's your best chance to get the toxic person in your workplace to stop doing whatever it is they're doing.

And it can be helpful if you are willing to bring this bad behavior to the attention of your other coworkers. You may be surprised to find out that there are one or a few coworkers—or maybe the entire team—who have had similar issues with this toxic person or are aware of the conflict. By having an open dialogue with coworkers, you are able to work together and address the issue at hand in order to make a positive change within the office.

While moving forward with the next steps, circle back to the Field Guide to the Sixteen Most Common Jerks at Work in Chapter 2 so that you are able to identify the kinds of characteristics and personalities of the most toxic coworkers. The following steps will help guide you through the process of calling out the bad behavior you're forced to encounter in the workplace.

1. IDENTIFY THE BAD BEHAVIOR

This first step is meant to help you identify the bad behavior that the toxic person at work is engaging in. In order to do this, take a look back at Chapter 2 to work through the different personality types and determine which type of toxic person you're dealing with. It's important to keep in mind that the person may be a hybrid, that is, they may embody more than one personality type. For example, they may be a mix of the Backstabber and the Lazy One.

Someone who behaves a certain way and has one of the toxic personalities might also engage in other bad behaviors that are represented more so in a different personality type. Once you identify those behaviors individually, then you can address them and get to the root of what's really going on. While you do this, maintain the 50,000-foot point of view in order to look at the person's behavior from an unbiased standpoint.

Case study. I work on the accounting team for our company, and tax season this past year was even more stressful than it usually is. I was rounding up all of our paperwork, expenses, and everything necessary to report our earnings for the year. We were approaching the deadline to submit our taxes, and I just needed to get some information about a few last-minute expenses to complete my task.

My coworker Jesse was the only one who had this information, so I emailed him about it. I even wrote "URGENT" in the subject line of the email—hoping that would get his attention and he would email the documents to me right away. He knew about our big deadline and that the company would be subject to penalties if the tax filing wasn't submitted by the deadline.

I waited one day for Jesse to respond, then when he didn't, I decided to email him again. I also texted him just in case for whatever strange reason, my email went to his spam inbox. The day came to an end, and I still hadn't heard from him. This was getting annoying and extremely stressful for me. I knew he was in the office, because he would occasionally respond to other group emails I was looped into.

I realized that I was dealing with someone who got some sort of pleasure out of not responding to others—especially when the need for response was urgent. He showed all the characteristics of that personality: he didn't seem to care about the needs of his coworkers, he was standoffish, absent, distracted, and most important, he didn't respond to my urgent request! It was helpful to figure out what kind of office jerk I was dealing with. It also made me feel like it wasn't me just overreacting—this was a real issue that I needed to sort out.

2. CONFRONT THE PERPETRATOR

Instead of just ignoring the behavior, letting it go, and allowing the toxic person to continue to do what he or she does, you must confront them. I know confrontation can be very difficult for a lot of people, especially when you're dealing with someone in a professional space, but it is necessary.

When you confront someone, this doesn't mean humiliating them in front of their coworkers, customers, or others. It means confronting them privately, one on one. Explain to the perpetrator what the bad behavior is that they are exhibiting, what you've observed, and express to them how much it personally affects you and the other people in the office. Tell them that you don't appreciate their behavior, you don't want them to continue it, and you don't want that behavior to be a part of your team any longer.

You don't have to make this one-on-one meeting a big, splashy deal. Rather, make it a low-key, relaxed meeting where you express your thoughts and feelings. When you address this person, do not yell or use an aggressive tone or language. Rather, go into it calmly but with assurance and confidence. Hear what they have to say—there may be valid reasons for their behavior. Or they may be unaware they are causing problems for you and others in your company and they may greatly regret their behavior. Whatever you do to confront this person, make sure you take steps to address the bad behavior.

Case study. In order to move forward with Jesse, and hope-fully be able to submit the company taxes on time, I needed to confront him. Since email clearly didn't get his atten-tion, I decided to go over to his office and pay him a visit. I knocked on his door, and he looked surprised to see me. I asked if I could come in, and he unenthusiastically nodded.

I entered his office and sat in the chair across from him. I didn't want to be aggressive about this—maybe there was a valid reason for Jesse's apparent inability to address my urgent request for information. I addressed his lack of response and how it was frustrating for me since I was responsible for submitting everything on time. I expressed to him the dire consequences of not turning in our taxes on time, and that it could potentially cost the company a lot of money in penalties. I didn't want to become overly pushy about him being non-responsive, but I definitely had to address those concerns, and that I needed his inputs right away.

After I finished my spiel, Jesse said, "I'll send those documents over to you right now." His response and apology sounded promising, and it seemed that he now understood that his lack of communication was impacting everyone at our company. I felt good about this, and I was looking forward to the change in Jesse's lack of responses.

3. PUSH BACK AS NECESSARY

In certain cases, you may need to push back against the behavior that a coworker is exhibiting, which goes beyond just confronting them or calling them out. You may have to actually actively push back. This means that when someone acts badly—a toxic person is doing their toxic thing to you—then don't be hesitant to call that person out.

For example, let's say you're in a meeting, and someone denigrates your contributions to a project and tries to make you look bad in front of the boss. Call out that behavior right then and there. You should never have to sit through a meeting with someone disrespecting you like that. The toxic person might say, "I think your idea is stupid and would never work; why can't you come up with a better idea?" Call out that person right then and there—don't let their bad behavior pass.

You should then ask them pointed questions about the motivation behind what they're trying to do. Ask, "Why are you trying to make me look bad in front of our manager?" "Why are you attacking me in front of the team?" Push back and challenge this person—don't let them think that this kind of toxic behavior is acceptable. Believe me—*everyone* will appreciate you for that.

Case study. The day after confronting Jesse, I still hadn't heard anything from him. It was so hard for me to understand why he was doing what he was doing, and not sending me the information that I needed. It didn't make sense to me at all.

Since it was Wednesday, we had our weekly meeting with the entire team. Each of us updated the team in turn, and I explained that I was working on the tax submission, which was due on Friday. Jesse was one of the last to give his updates. He blatantly lied, telling the team that we were working closely together on the taxes, and that they would be ready to be submitted soon.

I was taken aback, and pretty shocked when he said that. I decided to call him out on the false information he spread to the team. It would not be right for him to go unchallenged. I said, "Jesse, I've been waiting for days on important paperwork that only you have access to. I've sent you multiple emails with no response, and I even confronted you in person yesterday about the paperwork. I've been nothing but patient with you. Why haven't you sent me the paperwork yet?"

Jesse looked slightly taken aback and said that he would get the paperwork to me after the meeting. Of course, he made a dumb excuse about how he had been "too busy" and "caught up in other pressing tasks related to taxes." I know that despite how busy he was, he could have easily sent me the paperwork—it doesn't take long to upload a document and press the send button. It made me feel better that I was able to call him out in front of our coworkers. Hopefully he got the message and would change his behavior as a result.

4. DRAW A LINE IN THE SAND

In some cases, you may have to eventually draw the line in the sand. You have to decide how much of someone's toxic behavior at work you're willing and able to tolerate. We all have different levels of tolerance, and some toxic behaviors are worse than others. For example, someone who just grumbles and complains at a low level is not as egregious as someone who actively attacks you in front of your boss and tries to make you look bad so that they can steal a promotion that you are due for.

You have got to decide what *your* line in the sand is— how much bad behavior you are willing to put up with. I would recommend that you draw a line that is very clear to the people who are toxic in your office, and then make sure that once they step over the line, you do something about it. You should never just ignore it.

When the person crosses that line that you've drawn in the sand, there also needs to be some sort of consequence for their bad behavior. This is something you should think about—*what will the consequences be?* So, make sure that when you draw a line in the sand, you actually deliver some sort of consequence. If you don't, then they will surely test you again—and again, and again.

Case study. After the meeting, I realized that I was getting increasingly frustrated with Jesse's bad behavior. I ended up sending him a follow-up email directly after the meeting to remind him once again to send me the paperwork he had promised. I couldn't believe I was sending him—yet again—another email about this.

To my annoyance, I found myself refreshing my email to see whether or not Jesse had emailed me back. If he still did not send me the information by 4:00 p.m., I would have to visit his office again. This time, I needed to draw a line in the sand, and give him consequences for his lack of responsiveness and follow-through. I felt that if I didn't do this, he would continue with his non-responsive behavior.

Maybe if I went this route, I thought, he would finally feel like the stakes were high, and he would actually follow through with sending me what I needed. I thought about what my line in the sand consequences would be and I decided that if he didn't send it to me by tomorrow morning, I would have no other option but to bring our boss into this. She would want to know about my problems with Jesse so something could be done before the deadline for the tax submission.

As 4:00 p.m. slowly approached, and I still had not heard back from Jesse, I decided to go back to his office. I knocked and invited myself in—he didn't look too thrilled. I sat in the chair and told him the plan. He needed to send me the paperwork by 5:00 p.m. at the latest, and if he did not, then I had no other alternative than to loop our boss into this issue. I told him I didn't want it to reach that point, but if I had to, I would do it.

He acknowledged it, and apologized. He said that he would send it no later than 5:00 p.m. My hope and trust in Jesse had completely evaporated, and as I walked back to my office, I mentally prepared myself to discuss this with our boss. The rest of the day went by, and I still received nothing from Jesse.

5. AS A LAST RESORT, LOOP IN YOUR BOSS

I personally believe that whenever possible, you should try to deal with jerks at work yourself. You shouldn't go running to your boss every time there is a problem. The best thing you can do is to prevent your boss from having to deal with problems that you have with someone else in the office. I highly recommend that you confront and deal with these people yourself—yes, you have the power to do this.

When you try to confront them yourself, you are actively trying to solve and resolve the problem on your own. In some cases, however, no matter what line you draw in the sand, and no matter what consequences you offer, the person will just continue doing whatever it is they're doing that hurts you or others in the office. Perhaps they're getting some sort of pleasure out of making you or others in the office feel bad, or perhaps they're just oblivious to the toxic behavior they're engaging in.

If you can't get them to stop for whatever reason, and you've done all you can do, then go ahead and loop in your boss to explain what's going on. Allow your boss to play a role in neutralizing the toxic person in the workplace. Ask your boss for a private meeting, and go to their office to talk and explain to them the predicament you're in. Tell them who the person is and explain to them the toxic behavior that they're engaging in and how it is impacting you personally.

If it is impacting other coworkers, explain what kind of impact it is having on them as well, and the outcomes that the behavior has caused. *Is it causing people to be less engaged with their jobs? Is it causing people to talk about leaving their job and finding a more pleasant place to work? Is it causing productivity to decline?* Address any of the negative outcomes associated with the toxic person's behavior. Explain each of them to your boss, and then try to work with your boss to figure out how you can resolve this issue with the person causing the conflict.

Case study. I went to work extra early Thursday morning so that I could meet with my boss to tell her what was going on. I went to her office and sat in one of the chairs across from her. I told her that Jesse had been extremely unresponsive while I was working on the tax submission, and that I had sent him roughly twenty emails just asking him for this paperwork.

I brought up our Wednesday team meeting and how I thought it was terrible that he lied in front of everyone about how hard we had been working together—clearly, he was trying to cover up his own lack of teamwork and work ethic. I also mentioned that I had drawn a line in the sand

and offered Jesse one more chance before I approached our boss about it.

My boss seemed shocked by Jesse's behavior, and stressed that the taxes were due by tomorrow. They weren't complete yet and it was already Thursday. She immediately called Jesse and demanded that he come right away. Jesse walked in and sat in the chair next to mine. Our boss talked to us about the situation and told Jesse that his behavior was unacceptable.

Jesse opened up about how stressed and distracted he was in his personal life, and how he regretted that it had affected his professional life. He promised to be better at disconnecting the two, and when he was at work, to only focus on work. Our boss thanked him for his promise to do better in the future. However, Jesse needed to get me the expenses right now—there was no more time to waste.

Jesse apologized again, and our boss said she would schedule a one-on-one with Jesse once the taxes were submitted. I thanked both of them and went back to my office so I could get back to work. Five minutes later, I received the email from Jesse with the expense information I needed. Fifteen minutes later, I finished my task and got my report to accounting.

I'm glad I finally was able to get Jesse to submit the paperwork, although it was concerning that our boss had to be involved in order for him to actually send it to me. Hopefully this experience would help Jesse understand those boundaries he should have with work and personal life.

Of course, the success of looping in your boss assumes that you'll have their support. It's quite possible that you won't, and if that's the case, you'll need to try something different. This something different might include going over their head—to their boss—or in extreme situations, asking for a transfer to a different department, or perhaps even looking for a new position with a different employer. You'll have to decide which path is the best one for you, given your specific circumstances.

Don't ignore bad behavior, don't let it go on and on unaddressed or unchallenged. Make sure you do something about it. If it's a low-level conflict, then there is no need to worry about it unless it escalates further. If it is a high-level conflict that crosses the line you drew in the sand, then the issue has to be addressed no matter what. Use the steps in this chapter to address the situation head on and say something about it.

7

DON'T SWEAT THE SMALL STUFF

If small things have the power to disturb you, then who you think you are is exactly that: small.

—ECKHART TOLLE

Some bad behaviors—for example, sexual harassment—are *so* bad that they must be dealt with immediately, and decisively. Threats of physical or emotional harm must be dealt with immediately and decisively as well. However, there are many other bad behaviors that aren't really all that bad—for example, an employee who is five minutes late for a staff meeting once or twice a year. Being late to a meeting every once in a while is not all that big a deal, but if this increases to a couple of times a month or more, then it could be a problem.

It's important to keep in mind that we as humans make a mistake every once in a while. We make the wrong decision, we misjudge a situation, we hurt someone's feelings, and much more. Every single one of us has exhibited some number of minor bad behaviors at certain times throughout our careers, and it's important for us to be understanding of others' mistakes.

My advice is to avoid stressing out or being overly critical about a coworker's behavior unless it causes a significant, negative impact in the office. You should also avoid treating every bad behavior equally—bad behaviors have varying degrees of badness to them. In the same way as we think of the character types on a spectrum, think of bad behavior as a spectrum too, with zero being the smallest amount of bad behavior and ten being the largest amount of bad behavior. Depending on where someone's bad behaviors lie on the spectrum, you'll better understand whether you're facing a minor or major issue.

A lot of the time, these issues are minor. Choose your battles, and don't sweat the small stuff. As the old saying goes, don't make a mountain out of a molehill.

To assess the degree of bad behavior you're presented with and figure out whether you should stress about it or not, there are five essential steps you must take. Go through these carefully and remember to maintain that 50,000-foot viewpoint. It's important that your emotions don't get in the way of you being able to truly understand and assess the issue at hand. And keep in mind that other things in our lives—troubles at home, personal relationship issues, financial strain—may be stressing us out.

All this additional stress may make the minor actions of coworkers irritate us.

1. EXACTLY WHAT IS THE BAD BEHAVIOR?

The first thing you should do is take a close look at the behavior that seems toxic to you. Of course, it's bad enough that your coworker is engaging in this particular behavior in the first place, but what exactly is the behavior and how bad is it? Ask yourself questions that will help assess the level of "bad" that this behavior may be. Is it *really* that big of a deal? Why are you concerned about it? Is it having an impact on the organization, your team, or you personally?

For example, if a coworker is complaining about her job, are you personally being harmed? Is it a complaint you hear a couple times a month, or is it a complaint you hear a couple times a day? There's a big difference between the two. Is the person regularly stopping by your desk during work hours and bugging you for half an hour to complain about something? If so, then that's a big problem—for both of you. While it may make your coworker feel better, it takes away from your productivity and maybe even some of your satisfaction at work. But if it's an occurrence that happens just once in a while—say, in a public place in the office such as the lunchroom where they confide in you that they don't particularly enjoy their job—then what's the big deal?

If a coworker is infrequently exhibiting minor bad behavior and it isn't taking away from your own productivity or making you feel emotions that directly and negatively affect your ability to work or overall well-being, then it might be best for you to simply try to ignore it. Sure, you may feel annoyed, but with minor issues such as these, chances are your irritation will pass if you just allow it to.

Case study. I used to work with a woman who made me feel extremely uncomfortable. She would make strange sexual comments and physical advances that felt too close for comfort. It progressively became more and more of an issue, especially once she got my phone number. I would receive texts from her late at night that were definitely not PG. My coworker's behavior made me feel afraid to go into my office, and anxious that I'd have an unwanted confrontation with her. I didn't feel safe at my desk, or anywhere in the building for that matter.

As a result, I found myself getting distracted at work, and constantly looking up to make sure she wasn't staring at me or walking over to my desk. Her actions were most definitely not consensual, but I felt weird addressing this issue. *What if I was overreacting or something? What if this was all in my head?* I decided to assess what exactly her bad behavior was from a 50,000-foot viewpoint so that I could better understand it from an outside perspective and in case any sort of emotion was getting in the way.

I asked myself questions about how often she was doing this, how it impacted me, and how it impacted my team. I came to the conclusion that what she was doing was a serious issue that impacted my productivity, my relationships with others on the team, and my personal well-being. I felt violated, which is something no one should ever feel, and being in the office with her only made things more compli-cated. It wasn't just a minor annoyance—it was a big issue that was only getting worse and worse the longer I let her behavior go unchallenged.

2. IF IT'S A BIG DEAL, THEN CONFRONT THE PROBLEM

The moment you realize that the conflict you're dealing with at work is major, then you need to confront it. This means that the issue isn't just a minor annoyance—it has instead negatively impacted your productivity and well-being at work, and it is something that you can't and shouldn't have to tolerate. The behavior may be against company rules—or it might even be illegal.

Ask yourself: *What is the behavior? Is the behavior minor or major?* For example, if you've overheard an employee threaten a coworker with physical harm, then that's major and needs to be dealt with—*immediately.* Maybe they say they are going to assault the coworker in the parking lot after work if they don't do something that they want them to do. That's obviously a big issue. You should let your boss know right away and make sure that it's addressed. Take some notes to document the incidents—what exactly hap-pened and at what dates and times? Send or bring these notes to your boss so that it's clear what the situation is.

If someone threatens you with harm, you should let your boss know right away. This is something that needs to be dealt with immediately—not only for your own personal safety, but also the safety of the rest of the office.

In the previous chapter, we talked about drawing a line in the sand that the toxic person is aware of, and if they cross that line, there will be consequences. This is a perfect approach for major issues that rise above the level of mere annoyance. If the behavior becomes major, then it is something that you need to deal with—your coworker has crossed the line in the sand that you drew.

If your boss doesn't take your concerns seriously or does not act on them quickly or decisively, then you may need to go over their head—taking your concerns to your HR department or going to your boss's boss. While this may not make your boss very happy, you'll need to take action to ensure that the bad behavior is stopped. And if it's your boss that's doing the harassing, this puts you in an even more difficult situation.

Most companies have policies in place for reporting workplace sexual and other forms of harassment, whether it's instigated by your boss, your coworkers, or even customers or vendors. Be sure to follow your company's policies, which likely include documenting the harassment and filing a formal complaint.

If you've filed a complaint and no action is taken, then your company may be legally liable for allowing the harassment to continue. In that case, you may want to talk with a lawyer to see what your legal options are, or you may decide to look for a new job elsewhere. Whatever you decide, don't allow this bad behavior to continue. You have the power to stop it and you should use it.

Case study. Since I came to the conclusion that the sexually harassing behavior my coworker was engaging in was definitely major, I had to deal with it. I asked her to stop on several occasions—making it clear to her that the behavior was 100 percent unwelcome. However, my coworker continued to make sexually suggestive comments and physical advances, which meant I needed to get my boss in the loop and ask her to help.

This was extremely difficult for me to do since everyone in the office had strong working relationships with this woman, and they all loved and respected her. She had been at the company for a long time, and she was very well regarded. I didn't want to come across as being a narc, or overly sensitive about things that she did or said to me. But I was increasingly uncomfortable with her behavior and it was having a negative effect on my work.

I realized that inappropriate behavior is not okay in the workplace, no matter who does it. She overstepped my boundaries, and it should have been clear to her since I had already expressed that the feelings were not mutual, and I wanted her to stop. I stopped by my boss's office, closed the door, and asked for a few minutes of her time to discuss an important matter.

My boss was shocked to hear about my experiences with my coworker, but she was also very concerned for me. She took the matter seriously and asked for more information. I showed her screenshots of text messages my coworker had sent me and talked about instances that made me feel uncomfortable. She told me that this was not okay at all, and she was glad I spoke up—maybe there were others in the office who felt the same way.

She ensured that everything I said would be kept confidential, and that she would promptly talk with my coworker and demand an immediate change in her behavior for the better. If she was unable or unwilling to change her behavior, then there would be other consequences. It was a huge relief that my boss listened to me and that I wouldn't have to worry about my coworker's bad behavior again. I was still a little bit worried that the coworker would deny that she had done anything wrong, but I figured I would cross that bridge when I got there.

What happened after that was an even bigger surprise to me—my boss fired my coworker for her misbehavior. As it turned out, I wasn't the only target in the office and a couple other people revealed that they had also been harassed by the woman.

3. IF IT'S A LITTLE DEAL, THEN TRY TO IGNORE IT

If the issue is something that's not a big deal, then do your best to ignore it. There are several ways to help restrain yourself from turning a small issue into a big deal. Tuning it out is one option. You can choose to simply ignore their words or actions, excuse yourself, and walk away from the encounter.

This isn't always possible in certain instances, however. If the person is wandering into your office or workspace, annoying you, and taking up your time over something that isn't worth it, politely ask them to please take it elsewhere. Tell them that you have work to do and you need to focus on it, and that you really don't have time to listen to them complain about their problems.

Don't be shy to tell someone that you're busy and need to focus on your work. It's important that your productivity isn't altered by this person, regardless of who it may be— even your boss, or your boss's boss.

Case study. A few weeks after my coworker was fired, the office began to feel different. People weren't interacting as much with me, and everyone seemed to keep more to themselves. I knew my boss didn't tell anyone that I was the one who confronted her, but I couldn't help but think that someone must have figured out what happened and was actively spreading the rumor. It felt like people were intentionally avoiding me in the office. And when they did have to talk to me, the conversations tended to be short and uncomfortable.

One day, one of my coworkers, Jake, mustered up the courage to come up and ask me how I was doing, but also to pry about what had happened. It was clear he knew something, but not the whole story. I didn't want to say anything, so I tried to change the topic. After that, he would come up to me most every day and ask how I was doing, while simultaneously trying to ask about the situation.

His nosiness was bothering me a lot—it wasn't his place to know what happened anyway. He usually would come up to me when I was getting lunch or leaving the office for the day, so it never took away from my productivity at work. This was definitely a minor issue, but one that I still needed to address or else he'd continue to pry. I decided to tell him to leave it alone. Doing this stopped his constant check-ins, which I was very thankful for. This approach was very helpful in this situation.

4. FOCUS ON THE POSITIVE

Everybody has positives and negatives, and everybody has pluses and minuses. There are good aspects of people's personalities, and there are bad aspects as well. It's a normal thing that makes us human—no one on this planet is perfect and no one on this planet possesses only positive personality traits. There's always some negative in there too.

My suggestion is that you try to focus on the positive and find the positive things in the other person instead of looking at the negative. Sure, there may be some negatives that are a part of the person's overall package, but there are also probably a lot of positives that you enjoy. The person may be funny and keep the office light and happy. They may be an extremely productive worker with great customer service skills and customers love them. Maybe they're even the best barbecue cook at the company picnic every year. Whatever that positive is—being a great chef, being great with customers, being funny—focus on that positive as opposed to the negative attributes they may have. Look at the person as a whole, rather than fixating on a small part of them. Again, don't sweat it if it's not a big deal that is consistently impacting your productivity at work or mental well-being.

Case study. I was really disappointed by Jake's behavior. While he had backed off his constant prying into my personal business, he still asked me on occasion what I knew about our fired coworker. I would pick up on the little things he would do, and it seemed like every single thing would annoy me. His loud laugh, his wrinkled shirts, his talking during meetings—just about everything.

I was sad because I used to really like Jake, but his actions after the firing of our coworker really put me over the edge. I wanted to be able to be friends and work with Jake again, so I decided to stop fixating on his negative attributes. Not only was it making work unenjoyable for me, but it made me sad that I had lost a friend. It was clear that I hadn't thought about his positives in a while, and why we had been friends to begin with.

The positives I came up with: Jake was one of my first friends in the office and the first one to come up and introduce himself to me, he always went out of his way to make people feel comfortable, he always brought me coffee in the morning, he was funny, and he was genuinely nice and cared about people.

After thinking about his positives, I realized that they far outweighed the negatives I was fixated on. In fact, I felt as though my opinion of Jake had completely flipped, and I started to become less and less annoyed by his negative behaviors. In fact, none of those bad feelings about Jake seemed to matter anymore. Suddenly I felt sorry that I had become so fixated on his negatives. I hoped to be able to mend our personal and professional relationship.

5. CHANGE YOUR PERSPECTIVE

Consider that if you're obsessing over someone's minor, occasional toxic behaviors and you're ignoring the major positive behaviors, maybe it's *you* who needs a change in perspective. If you are nitpicking over small details of someone's personality, that's not a good thing and it can be toxic to other coworkers. Maybe by actively changing your perspective, and deciding to stop worrying about it, everything will turn out okay. Maybe the workplace will be a better place for everyone—including *you*.

Changing your perspective will allow you a clearer viewpoint on the situation and your coworker. You may even realize things about yourself that you are able to work on in order to better yourself, and your relationships with others.

Case study. Since I had been obsessing about Jake's behavior, I also decided that I should look more deeply into my own thought process and think of the reasons I may have been so sensitive to people recently. I wanted to change my perspective—not only when it came to my opinions about Jake, but also my perception of others in the office. Since I had felt a strange distance between me and my other coworkers since the incident, I wanted to fix this.

I reflected on the past few weeks, and how I really did go through a lot. I was worried about what others would think of me and I was worried that they would end up not liking me if they felt that I was to blame for our coworker being fired. I realized that I was placing myself in a bubble—not letting anyone in out of fear of rejection and hurt feelings. In reality, all of these worries were just in my head. I was scared of what others were thinking, and because I was afraid, my normal interactions with coworkers changed. I was the one avoiding people, not the other way around.

Once I realized all of this, I noticed that all of my interactions with my coworkers the past few weeks had been colored by my own negative, self-conscious viewpoint. I actively needed to change my perspective and actions in the office in order for things to go back to the way they were before my boss fired the harassing coworker. Once I did this, things went back to normal more quickly than I expected.

I ended up confiding in Jake about what had happened, and he was very supportive. He apologized for being so nosey, and he explained that that was his way of trying to help me sort out my feelings and thoughts. He wanted to talk me through it and make sure I was okay—he could sense how uncomfortable I appeared around everyone in the office.

I started going to lunch and interacting with coworkers again, and I finally felt comfortable at the office for the first time in a long while. By changing my perspective on the situation, I was able to understand the reasons for my feelings of being uncomfortable in our office. I was the one inflicting toxic behavior in the workplace—not only with my coworkers but with myself as well. I made sure to not cast all of the blame on myself since I had just come out of an abusive situation with another coworker. But it was also important for me to realize that I needed to assess and change my own perspective when I was having a conflict.

There are many different kinds of conflicts that can happen in the office. In general, some issues are big, and some issues are small. These issues all have varying degrees of "bad." Sometimes we fixate too much on the small things, when we only really need to deal with the big stuff so that things don't continue in the direction they're going and progressively worsen. If these conflicts are ones that will potentially put someone in harm's way either psychologically or physically, those are the conflicts that need to be addressed and taken care of as soon as possible. If a conflict is more of an annoyance that doesn't hurt you physically or mentally, and it is something that can easily be avoided, that is a small conflict.

If it's small, don't sweat it.

FUTURE-FOCUSED MINDFULNESS

Is your mind still? Are you able to give your full attention to the present moment, or do you find yourself giving in to your anxieties instead? If you're constantly faced with a busy mind and don't know how to deal with your emotions in healthy ways, you may want to consider mindfulness.

Described as paying attention to the present moment without judgment, mindfulness works as an effective method for reducing stress and bolstering health.

Though mindfulness and meditation practices have existed for thousands of years, the business world has taken a recent liking to these techniques, as they have been proven to strengthen focus and concentration, regulate emotions, and improve leadership and collaboration skills.

It is true that mindfulness asks that you concentrate on the current moment, but this practice actually goes beyond just the present experience. In fact, a future-focused mindfulness, which focuses on what is to come, can be just as powerful for the business leaders of today.

Future-focused mindfulness requires an effective navigation of the future, necessary for your long-term success. When your future-oriented mindset is tied to mindfulness, you will become familiar with *prospection*, which involves "mentally generating (prospecting for, discovering, creating) future possibilities and options." This helps you see all the probabilities that are before you, so you may change paths or moves as needed.

Plus, rather than doing something that will prove to be harmful for your future, you will select the options that instead improve your future, because you are mindful of their existence and can adapt accordingly. As Thomas Bateman explains in a *Psychology Today* article, "For individuals, leaders, and societies, such future-focused adaptation is what it means to be truly proactive."[8]

Concentrate deeply on each sensation of the future, as well as that of the here and now if you desire serious professional and personal growth. Being mindful of your future means being mindful of the actions you take today—the very same actions that will undoubtedly have a profound impact on your tomorrow!

No matter which type of mindfulness method you practice, it's always a good time to listen to the wisdom of Mother Teresa, who once advised, "Be happy in the moment, that's enough. Each moment is all we need, not more."

8

LEARN BY NEGATIVE EXAMPLES

It is important to expect nothing, to take every experience, including the negative ones, as merely steps on the path, and to proceed.

—RAM DASS

In every workplace, there's always someone who's a jerk—maybe even multiple jerks. It's just a fact of life: in your personal and work life, there will always be people who try to tear you down instead of building you up. These people are certainly never great to be around either. They're not pleasant to be with and working with them usually turns out to be a significantly negative experience. They can demoralize a team, they can damage relationships, and they can reduce productivity and employee engagement.

Although there are plenty of negative aspects to these toxic people, let's think for a moment about what good can come out of this. Instead of becoming disheartened by the negative, toxic people at work, there are some very valuable and long-lasting lessons you can learn by observing these people. By observing them, you'll be able to understand what kinds of behaviors you might yourself engage in that are hurting the people, teams, and customers you're working with.

Think about it: By seeing what others are doing wrong, you can learn to refrain from engaging in their bad behaviors. As we observe, we're sure to catch ourselves doing some of the same things that these office jerks are doing. By catching ourselves, we are able to learn how we can stop that toxic behavior before it becomes a big issue. And, even better, the education you receive from your toxic coworkers is completely free of charge—their behavior will be demonstrated in front of you every day at work whether you like it or not. When you've seen and experienced these negative examples firsthand, you'll learn valuable lessons.

You'll learn what not to do in the workplace and what behaviors you should not engage in if you want your office to be the best possible place it can be for you and people you work with. Learning from bad coworkers can be just as important as learning from good coworkers. By watching and observing others, you'll gain a better understanding of navigating and working with people, as well as educating yourself on how you should act.

In order to utilize your office jerk experience to your fullest advantage, there are five points here that you should consider. By going through these steps, you will be able to understand what kind of office jerk your coworker is, how you can navigate their behavior, and how you can actively make smart choices about your own behavior.

We all partake in bad behavior at one point or another, so in order to understand how we can fix our own toxic habits, it's helpful to strategically analyze fellow coworkers who may exhibit bad behavior. Please take a moment right now to observe the negative behaviors of those around you and what lessons you can learn from them. You might be surprised.

1. FIGURE OUT WHO THE JERKS ARE IN YOUR ORGANIZATION

Offices are typically pretty diverse when it comes to the different kinds of personality types, and chances are you know exactly who the toxic people are in your office. These are the ones who can't seem to help themselves from being a jerk at almost every and any opportunity. These people will generally continue to engage in their behavior until they are confronted—either by the person who is the target of their toxicity, or by their boss. And if for some reason they haven't been confronted or otherwise dealt with, you'll continue to see the toxic behavior of these coworkers throughout your time with the organization. So, if you don't know who these people are now, you're sure to find out at some point.

That said, some jerks at work are pretty stealthy in their behavior. They're experts at staying under the radar— barely being noticed as they create havoc among your coworkers. And sometimes the toxic behaviors they engage in are at a low level and you may not notice them at first.

So, in order to understand exactly who it is you're working with, one of the most reliable approaches is also one of the easiest: just ask your coworkers. Your coworkers have had to deal with these toxic individuals for quite some time and they know who they are. They may even have tips for working with specific people that can be beneficial to you. By asking coworkers you trust, you'll know exactly who the toxic people are at work, and you will also learn how you can try to productively work with them.

Case study. I was new to my office, and like many newbies, I really didn't know the lay of the land yet. This wasn't my first job, so I had already anticipated that there would be at least one or two coworkers I should keep my distance from or learn to work with. The first week at a new place is always kind of crazy—you're constantly meeting new people left and right, trying to remember names and faces. To the best of my ability, I made a note of everyone I met and paid careful attention to the way other coworkers acted around specific people, and vice versa.

After I had made my introductions, I reflected on my first impressions of everyone I met. Sometimes you can get a feeling about people—those who are especially nice and those who aren't. This was the first time that I really couldn't sense anything that felt off for anyone I had met that week. I became close to one of my coworkers, Sasha. She helped me navigate the office and feel at home. We quickly became friends.

Since I couldn't get a good understanding of who the toxic people in the office might be, I decided to ask Sasha about her experiences with our coworkers. I trusted her and felt that she would be open and candid with me. She pointed out a guy in our department named Chad who had earned a reputation for constantly wanting to be in the spotlight and taking the credit for other coworkers' work. She said that he had been an especially frustrating person to work with.

Sasha also mentioned that a woman in our department named Jessica was a big talker. She told me that Jessica would talk your ear off about non-work-related things at just about any hour of the day—everything from her favorite TV shows to her political leanings. It was difficult to focus on work sometimes because she would interrupt anyone anytime, no matter what they were doing or what kinds of deadlines they were working under.

After talking to Sasha about her thoughts and experiences with these coworkers, I had a much better idea of who exactly the potentially toxic coworkers were in the office so I could learn how to navigate them.

2. TAKE A CLOSE LOOK AT THE BEHAVIORS THAT MAKE THEM JERKS

When there's a jerk in the office that you're well aware of, you have to really dig into who they are and what it is they're doing that makes them a jerk. Take the time to note their characteristics—things you noticed that may seem off, personal experiences people have shared with you, and anything else that can relate to their toxic behavior. Ask yourself questions such as, *What exactly are they doing that's toxic? What kinds of behaviors are they choosing to engage in?*

For example, are they complaining all the time? Are they putting other people down? Are their egos so huge that they always want to shine a spotlight on themselves and not others? What are these different behaviors, and how do they affect everybody on your team? Are they always coming from the perspective of a glass half-empty or a glass half-full? Get a feel for what behaviors they're engaging in and catalog them.

As you take note of what their behaviors are, you will start to understand who they are as a person. And once you understand who they are as a person, you will start to learn how you're able to maneuver working with these specific types of personalities.

Case study. Now that Sasha had told me about two of the people in the office who had exhibited toxic behavior, I wanted to take a closer look at these individuals. Throughout the next few days, I went out of my way to observe and interact with both Jessica and Chad. I wanted to understand their behaviors and try to pick up on what Sasha had told me to beware of.

After spending time with them, I think I had a pretty good understanding of their toxic behaviors. I decided to write each of their characteristics down on a notepad so I could take a close look at who they really are. For Jessica, the characteristic observations I wrote down were: talkative, distracted from her work, shallow, likes to be the center of attention, not self-aware—she doesn't get it when people are disinterested in what she has to say.

I thought about what exactly it was that made Jessica toxic, and I came to the conclusion that it was indeed her talkative behavior. She talked excessively and it became very distracting from work. I wasn't sure why she engaged in this behavior—if it was her way of taking a break from the work she had to do, or if it was because she wanted to be the center of attention. There was no specific topic she would talk about—it ranged from what she ate for lunch, to an assignment she was working on, to the podcast she listened to while driving to work.

For Chad, the characteristics I wrote down were: constantly talks about his accolades, enjoys being the center of attention, uses "I" when presenting a team project instead of "we." Based on my observations, I could definitely tell that everything had to revolve around him, and that he claimed the work of others, which I could see just simply by his choice of wording. He would always say "I did this" versus "we did this."

This was something that I could tell bothered people a lot and started to bother me the more I worked with and observed him. Writing a list of characteristics that I had observed for both Chad and Jessica was a helpful way of organizing my thoughts and feelings about their toxic behavior.

3. COMPARE THEM TO THE FIELD GUIDE IN CHAPTER 2

In this next step, you will need to consult the Field Guide to the Sixteen Most Common Jerks at Work in Chapter 2 in order to really figure out what kind of jerk you're working with. Each of the sixteen problem personality types are distinct and represent a different kind of person. By going through this exercise, you will learn about how to best deal with these people at work.

When you think of the person in your office you're trying to pinpoint and understand better, ask yourself questions that correlate with each of the sixteen personality types.

- *Are they pessimistic?*
- *Do they have the magic ability to see the flaws in just about everything?*
- *Are they naturally cynical about any outcome and situation?*
- *Are they envious—do they envy everyone's good fortune and success?*
- *Do they always want what someone else has?*
- *Do they talk too much behind other people's backs?*
- *Are they an intimidator—aggressive with their coworkers to get what they want?*
- *Do they manipulate others by threatening them and ridiculing them?*

Case study. After I wrote down the characteristics I observed in both Jessica and Chad, I wanted to get a better grasp of the specific toxic personalities that they embodied so I could further understand who they really were and how I could best deal with them. As I sifted through a variety of different personality types, I decided on the types that matched my two coworkers the best.

I came to the conclusion that Jessica was the Chatter and Chad was the Credit Thief (and possibly the Narcissist as well, but I couldn't be so sure yet based on my observations). Jessica was friendly and social, she talked more than anyone else in the room, she enjoyed being the center of attention, she never ran out of things to talk about, and she definitely lacked self-awareness. She just didn't realize the harm she was doing to her organization.

Chad's behavior, on the other hand, was aligned with the Credit Thief. He typically slacked off and was confident, a good liar, could be nice and enjoyable to be around, loved being in the spotlight, thrived on accolades and praise— even if it wasn't rightfully his.

Now that I was able to pinpoint what type of toxic coworkers Jessica and Chad were, I felt more confident about being able to tolerate their behavior and work with them for the foreseeable future.

4. LEARN LESSONS FROM THE FIELD GUIDE IN CHAPTER 2

In the field guide in Chapter 2, there are case studies pertaining to each character type. These case studies explain a different scenario of someone being toxic in the workplace, and how a coworker learned lessons from dealing with their office jerk. You can look at each of these case studies and learn lessons from the people who were involved— from the perspective of the perpetrator who is engaged in the bad behaviors, and the perspective of the victim who has learned how to deal with the toxic person.

By reading through these different case studies, you will be able to put yourself in the shoes of the coworker who has to deal with the office jerk and learn from their experience—how it made them feel and how it negatively impacted their work and other coworkers. You will be able to utilize these lessons in your own lived experiences at work.

Case study. As I considered the behavior that Jessica engaged in, I found that I personally related to the situation quite a bit—especially since I was a new employee who fell victim to the Chatter's ways. This person typically is nice and likeable, and when you're a new hire who hasn't yet built any relationships, any friend at the office is warmly welcomed. But when this person talks so much that it gets in the way of your productivity, that's when it becomes an issue.

In the case of Chad—the Credit Thief—I could clearly see that he would present assignments and projects like they were solely his and there was no one else on the team who helped him. Fortunately, I wasn't one of the team members whose credit was taken by Chad—at least not yet—but there was a very good chance that this would happen in the future if I was assigned to work with him on a project.

Reflecting on the personality types driving the behavior of these two coworkers helped inform the way I viewed them and how I could prepare myself for working with Chad on a collaborative project or telling Jessica to leave me alone if her chatting became too much. I knew that Chad and Jessica were not the only Credit Thieves and Chatters I would work with during the course of my career, so I figured it would be useful to consider this as a golden opportunity for a learning experience.

5. AVOID DOING WHAT THE JERKS IN YOUR ORGANIZATION DO

As I've mentioned in previous chapters, we all have a little bit of office jerk in us. Some more than others, but however much it is, we can prevent ourselves from becoming the office jerk that we don't like to work with. In order to do this, you must become self-aware of your own behaviors and what you might be doing that is toxic to others. Maybe your behavior is only causing a minor problem; however, that minor problem is still preventable if you act upon it.

When you go through the characteristics and examples of the office jerks in Chapter 2, take note of what exactly it is that these office jerks are doing. Whatever the bad behaviors are that they're engaging in are behaviors that you don't necessarily want to engage in yourself. The best way to avoid becoming a jerk in the office is to avoid embodying those specific characteristics listed in the field guide.

Also take note of what other coworkers are doing that are toxic, and refrain from doing the same thing that they're doing. If you have a bad coworker, don't stoop down to their level and form their habits that you've seen as toxic. We'll address this in more depth in the next chapter (Chapter 9), but make sure to not do the same things that these office jerks are doing.

Case Study. As I reflected on their behavior, I noticed that I also had several characteristics and habits that Jessica and Chad possessed. While I didn't consider myself to be a toxic person in any way, I came to the conclusion that I did have some things to work on. I didn't want to be like Jessica or Chad, so the farther I could get from becoming like them, the better.

I realized, for example, that I had a bad habit of talking to coworkers when I needed a distraction from work. I never thought that this could actually be hurting their productivity, but I'm sure in certain cases it did. I was nowhere near the chattiness of Jessica but talking to others was a way for me to take a break from work. Don't get me wrong, taking breaks at work is a healthy thing to do, but not at the expense of other coworkers' productivity.

I actively made a mental note to stop saying "I" so much, and instead say "we" when it was the team together that accomplished something. Or if it was a project that I did solely, I could make an effort to connect my successes to the team as a whole. If we're a team, any success I have is also a collaborative success. I became very sensitive to "I" phrases because I wanted to be the opposite of Chad—a coworker who people didn't like working with.

Having both Jessica and Chad as coworkers was actually a very big learning experience for me, and hugely beneficial for other experiences I've had with different people. They helped me understand who I want to be in the office, and who I don't want to be. This will be something I carry with me throughout the rest of my career.

Overall, you can learn a lot from the negative people in your life. Sure, you can learn how to be a good person, a good worker, and a good boss by watching the examples of good people who you work with. But you can also learn valuable lessons from watching the negative behaviors of the toxic people you work with and by making sure that you aren't also exhibiting the same toxic behavior that they are. Utilize your experiences with these toxic coworkers and learn from them. These experiences throughout your career will be immensely helpful as you continue to work with different people with different personalities.

9

DON'T BE A JERK YOURSELF

*It isn't the ups and downs that make
life difficult; it's the jerks.*

—CHARLIE CHAPLIN

No book about jerks at work would be complete without a little bit of self-assessment. Take a good look at yourself then answer this question: Are *you* a jerk at work?

Are you *sure*?

If you're not so sure about your own status and what your coworkers think of you, simply ask them. Some businesses routinely administer confidential 360-degree surveys that can provide employees (especially managers) with honest and unvarnished feedback from those who work with them. It may seem intimidating to be vulnerable and to encourage feedback from others that might turn out to be a blow to your ego, but it can be remarkably useful.

As I mentioned earlier, we all have a little bit of jerk in us, no matter how "good" we are—or how "good" we think we are. We may sometimes be just a bit too talkative at work, or maybe we gossip about other coworkers occasionally, or maybe we slack off one or two times too often each month. Just like reaching for an ice cream cone instead of a stalk of broccoli for dessert, it's simply human nature to cave to some toxic behaviors once in a while. So, don't be too hard on yourself if you catch yourself being a bit of a jerk from time to time.

The best thing you can do is to acknowledge your bad behavior, try to minimize it in the future, and move on with your life. By doing this, you will become an overall better coworker and employee. If you don't want others to be jerks at work, then you should set a positive example for others to follow. In an ideal situation, everyone at the office will evaluate their behaviors, and work toward obliterating whatever it is they do that is toxic. In this way, everyone will set positive examples for one another, leading to a better work environment.

Now, you might be asking yourself, *How can I tell if I'm a jerk? How can I find out if I am actually a toxic person and contributing toxicity to my workplace?*

Well, in order to do this, you're going to have to welcome vulnerability with open arms, and really pull down your guard. In order to assess your actions and figure out whether or not you're being a jerk at work, one of the best and most effective things you can do is to ask coworkers about their perception of you. This may sound unappealing in many ways, but it's a challenge that will only make you stronger. By taking authority over this situation, and really working on yourself, you will help make your office a better work environment for everyone.

In order to find out if you are a contributing factor to potential issues in the workplace, let's consider five specific steps you can take. It may be difficult to be completely vulnerable with your coworkers but doing so will make a tremendous difference in the results you obtain. Keep this in mind as you go through each step that will help you become the best employee and coworker you possibly can be.

1. ASSESS HOW PEOPLE ACT AROUND YOU

You probably know through your own experiences that, when someone is toxic to you or to others you work with, your natural first reaction is usually to avoid them. And, as I previously explained, when someone is engaging in toxic behavior, it's always a good idea to take a step back to evaluate the interaction and then decide how to proceed. The question here is, how are people acting around *you*? Not sure? Ask yourself questions such as, *How are people at work acting around me? Are some of my coworkers trying to avoid me? Who and when?*

If people are acting weird around you or are trying to avoid you and stay out of your way, there's probably a good reason. That good reason might be that you're acting like a jerk at work. So, take a good look at how the people around you are interacting with you. Are they trying to avoid meeting with you? Are they trying to avoid hanging out with you during lunch, after work, during meetings, or just walking down the hallway? Do they say a quick hello and run off to try and disappear? Or do they actually hang out with you and genuinely want to spend time with you? If people are avoiding you, that's probably a pretty good sign that you're being toxic at work—even just a little bit—and you should take a closer look at your behaviors.

Case study. After having dealt with a few toxic coworkers throughout my career, I wanted to understand whether or not I had my own toxic tendencies as well. Many people who exhibit bad behavior at work typically don't realize the impact that they're having or that their behavior is even bad.

The first thing I did was observe and reflect on how people had been interacting with me at work. I never had any close friends in the office, but I didn't think I was on bad terms with anyone either. I kind of just assumed this was typical office behavior. I went throughout my normal workday, occasionally saying brief hellos to people I encountered throughout the day. One thing that hit me was that I never really had any in-depth conversations with people, and I noticed that others in my office actually seemed to hang out together and have fun. They even sometimes got together outside of work for a drink or other activities.

I never thought of this as peculiar until I realized just how left out I was compared with my other coworkers. Since I didn't have any real relationship with anyone in the office, this made me realize that I must be doing something to rub people the wrong way. I had to investigate further.

2. GET FEEDBACK FROM OTHERS

It's one thing to notice that people are avoiding you or acting sort of strange around you, but you can actually get more information by asking for feedback from others. If you notice specific people who are actively avoiding you, ask the person, "Is there something I've done? Is there something going on that is causing you to avoid me?" Ask for candid feedback and let the person know that you genuinely want to improve the way that you're behaving at work. You're trying to improve yourself, and you're not trying to get back at them—you aren't going to use their words against them.

When your coworkers provide their honest feedback, they will help you improve the way you act in the office, which can make things better for them too. Tell them you really want to improve and that you sincerely want their unvarnished, honest feedback. As long as someone feels safe giving you feedback—and most likely they will—this can turn out to be a very positive thing.

If they feel unsafe and they feel like you're going to get back at them in some way or punish them for providing you with their honest opinion, then they probably won't bother. If your coworker asks *you* for unvarnished feedback, be honest with it—it will not only be beneficial to you, but it will be beneficial for the entire team. We all need to be and can be better at work, and to ensure that we're not being toxic to ourselves and others, we need to be vulnerable and listen to the feedback we receive.

Case study. I decided it was time to approach a few of my coworkers and ask them for their candid feedback. I was nervous to do this—I don't particularly like being called out on things, and it's hard for me to be completely vulnerable with people. Let's just say I'm not great when it comes to constructive criticism.

When I went up to the first coworker for feedback, I was honestly quite anxious. And when I asked her for her candid feedback, she looked pleasantly surprised. She even had to state the question back to me to make sure she had understood my question correctly. She lightly laughed, and said, "Well, you're kind of self-obsessed. You never make a point to ask how we're doing, or how we feel. Sometimes I feel like you think we're subordinates and dumber than you. To be quite frank, it's not very enjoyable to work with someone who appears to think they're better than everyone else."

Her words came as a shock to me. *Was I that self-obsessed?* I knew that I was confident in myself, and I knew my capabilities were pretty high, but I didn't think that my confidence would come across as narcissism. I thanked her for being honest and let her know that I was seeking out more coworkers for feedback that day. The more people I talked to, the more it became clear that I had an issue. People didn't seem to enjoy my presence because of how self-absorbed I was. They felt that I was arrogant and only cared about myself.

This is something I had to fix. I knew the importance of everyone feeling comfortable when working with a team of people, and I didn't want to be that one bad coworker who made everyone else feel uncomfortable.

3. TAKE THE FEEDBACK YOU GET FROM OTHERS SERIOUSLY

Once you get feedback from your coworkers, it's important that you take it seriously, and that you don't just ignore it and throw it out. This is especially true when you're hearing the same feedback from more than one person. Certainly, if one person gets upset at you for some reason, but everyone else in the office doesn't seem to have a problem with you and isn't avoiding you, then that one person's feedback may indicate that you two just don't get along. So, when you do get a decent amount of feedback from more than one person saying that you have a toxic streak and you're a bit of a jerk at work, then you should take that feedback quite seriously and act on it immediately.

There's another benefit to taking the feedback of others seriously besides the fact that you'll have a better chance of improving. When people see that you take their feedback seriously, then they will be more willing to offer it. They will also be more appreciative of you and your efforts with changing your ways. If you don't take their feedback seriously, they won't bother giving you any more, and you won't benefit one bit from it. It's really in your best interest to take your coworkers' feedback seriously.

Case study. When I got home from work, I wrote down what my coworkers had said to me that day. The things that stood out and became clear to me all added up to one inescapable conclusion: that I was participating in some degree of toxic behavior that was detracting from the efforts of my team. I wrote down words and phrases such as *narcissistic, self-absorbed, confident, can never be wrong, asserts opinion too much, only talks about myself, arrogant.* It hurt to write these words out and know that these were the characteristics that my coworkers saw in me. According-ing to these attributes, I wouldn't want a coworker like me either.

This was the most vulnerable I had ever been around anyone in a professional space—it was frightening to me, but it was clearly very important. Learning about all of this changed my perspective on myself and made me motivated to change. I wanted to change my behavior so that my team would be the best it could possibly be. I regret waiting so long to ask my coworkers about how they felt about me. Better late than never though.

4. SET A GOAL

Once you have received feedback that you're exhibiting toxic behavior at work, and you're not behaving as well as you should be, you have to set a goal. You need to actually put your coworkers' feedback into action. For example, if you're the Envier—someone who envies other people's accomplishments and tries to shoot their successes down—then set a goal to quit engaging in that negative behavior. Stop looking at others' accomplishments as a blow to your own ego and sense of self-worth, be happy about what you've accomplished at work, and be happy for your coworkers' successes as well.

Put yourself in their shoes. If there was someone who shut down every accomplishment you had, and was never happy for you—how would that make you feel? Probably not very good. If someone achieves a difficult assignment or gets a big promotion, then be happy for them. Celebrate them for achieving that really difficult goal. If one of your coworkers is congratulated or praised in a meeting by your boss for doing something great at work, congratulate them for that. After the meeting, go up to them and say "Good job," and how proud you are of them. You don't need to shoot them down, you don't need to undercut them. In fact, it's ultimately not in your best interest to do that. Take the time to set a goal and actually put the feedback into action and take positive steps that help you achieve that goal.

Let me tell you about my friend, Adam Kreek. An entrepreneur and motivational speaker, Adam is a guy who knows a lot about setting goals. Not only did he and his rowing team win a gold medal for Canada at the 2008 Beijing Olympic Games, but he and three other rowers came within a few days of successfully rowing across the Atlantic Ocean. Sadly, their boat capsized seventy-three grueling days after they left the shores of Africa.

We're all familiar with the timeworn idea of SMART goals: specific, measurable, attainable, relevant, and timebound. According to Adam, today's businesses need new ways of setting goals, and CLEAR goals do just that. CLEAR goals are:

Collaborative: Goals encourage employee teamwork and collaboration. Ask yourself: *With whom? Who is on my team? Who supports my team? Who is my team serving? Who are the stakeholders? Customers? Who in power do I need on my team? Which employees, colleagues can help? Who do I need above me? Who do I need below me? Who do I need alongside me? Why do these collaborators matter?*

Limited: Goals are limited in both duration and scope. Ask yourself: *When do I start? When do I stop? What geographical limits exist? What personal limits exist? Am I being realistic? How will I know when the goal is complete? Is there anything that I should not do to achieve this goal?*

Emotional: Employees are emotionally connected to the goals. Ask yourself: *Does this goal serve my purpose? Does this goal feed my needs? Why am I doing this? Am I 100 percent dedicated to this goal's outcome? How will my goal affect the emotions of the people I manage? The people who manage me? My teammates? How will this goal affect my personal goals and career plans?*

Appreciable: Large goals can be broken down into smaller goals so they can be accomplished more quickly and easily for long-term gain. Ask yourself: *What is the next, smallest, most-obvious action? What key performance indicators can I use for metrics? What key milestones exist in the achievement of this goal? What other goals will be* *accomplished on the road to accomplishing this goal? What objectives can I stack and track?*

Refinable: Be flexible and agile, and give yourself permission to refine and modify your goals as necessary, even if they're set with a headstrong objective. Ask yourself: *What information can I anticipate changing? What (beyond my control) could cause the above not to occur? Would a change in path mean a change in my highest goals? What matters most? When will I revisit this goal to tweak it? What is most likely to go wrong? How will I adapt to the best-case scenario, worst-case scenario, and most-likely scenario?*

Back to our story: Adam explains,

> When we prepared for our Atlantic crossing, our higher goal was to cross the Atlantic Ocean, but we also created three rules to support that higher goal. The first rule was don't die, the second rule was don't kill your mates, and the third was don't sink your boat. So, look after yourself, look after each other, and look after your equipment.

We can apply Adam's CLEAR goal-setting method when we are setting a goal for changing our toxic behavior at work.

Case study. Now I was very motivated to change my behavior and prove to my coworkers that I wasn't the full-blown narcissist they thought I was. Broadly, my goal would be to stop being so narcissistic. I knew it would be hard to completely change my ways, so this goal felt daunting—especially since I honestly had no idea that I was prone to this behavior until recently. I needed time to go through what exactly my goal was, how it was beneficial, and how I could achieve it.

I decided to go through the CLEAR goals in order to fully walk through what exactly it was that I was trying to achieve.

Collaborative: Why was my team important in this matter? They had helped me understand the toxic behaviors I was exhibiting, which I truly couldn't have done on my own. Now I just needed to prove to them that I was able to change for the better. Throughout my journey of throwing out my narcissistic tendencies, I knew that I would need their support and honest feedback so that I knew that I was on the right track. My goal was very much collaborative in every way. If I was not improving, and no one addressed it with me, then my goal would not be met.

Limited: I had to set a specific time frame for myself to achieve this goal. I wanted to start right away, so I decided that I would begin the next day at work. Since it is difficult to change old habits that you have grown used to, I gave myself a month to complete it. By the end of the month, I wanted to completely obliterate my narcissistic tendencies. In order to know whether or not I completed my goal towards the end of the month,

I would check in with my coworkers and get a new round of evaluations from them every week. Hearing their feedback was essential to understanding whether I completed my goal or not.

Emotional: I needed to consider how this goal would be beneficial to both me and my team, and how it would make a positive impact. This goal would help me become the best coworker and employee I could possibly be. My relationships with people would be better, and the way I work with people would be more collaborative. In the past, I had rubbed people the wrong way, created tension, and people didn't want to work with me. By changing my behavior, I would be helping others in the office feel more comfortable in our workspace, which would hopefully cause better productivity and less tension. I wanted to be friends with people, and I wanted to be able to work with coworkers in the most collaborative, high-achieving way possible. By following this goal, and tapping deep into my own emotions, I sincerely hoped I would be able to accomplish all this.

Appreciable: Since I was tackling a hefty goal, it was helpful to break it down a bit. As my first achievable action, I wanted to stop frequently using "I" statements while talking to my team. This seemed like an attainable goal, and one that coworkers on my team would be able to quickly notice. I also wanted to start by complimenting others' ideas and successes so that

I could get rid of the elitist, self-absorbed demeanor that my coworkers had mentioned. Throughout the course of doing this, I asked for weekly feedback from my coworkers, and in turn, I hoped that this would bring me closer to them. I hoped that their active participation in my journey to undoing my toxic behavior would make our relationships stronger.

Refinable: As with everything in life and business, the world constantly changes around us. I wanted to prepare just in case I needed to alter the way I was going about my goal. The biggest thing that could arise is people being confused by my sudden change and feeling as though I'm not doing this for them. Since I had already come across to my coworkers as narcissistic, they might think that my actions would only benefit me, and in the long run would work against them in some way. I needed to prepare for that. People might be skeptical about my intentions and that was okay—I was there to prove them wrong.

Halfway through the month, I wanted to reflect on all of the weekly feedback I had received, and write my goals moving forward into the rest of the month. If there were things that I was still lacking in, I would shift my energy into focusing on changing those things. I listened to anything that my coworkers said, and my trajectory was subject to change depending on their feedback. I went into my month-long goal prepared to be flexible, vulnerable, and trusting of the process.

5. FOLLOW THROUGH

Once you've set goals and worked toward achieving them, you'll want to follow through to make sure that you actually stopped behaving in the bad ways that you have been trying to change. That means going back out and looking at how people are reacting to you. Are they still trying to avoid you, or are they now engaging with you and inviting you to go to lunch or to hang out after work with them? Are they sitting next to you at meetings, and not trying to sit as far away as humanly possible?

Take another look and see if people's behavior towards you has changed. If it has—if they're being more welcoming and there is less noticeable avoidance—that's great. It means you're doing something right and you're on the way to achieving your personal goals.

Again, go back out for feedback. Schedule time to sit down and meet with people in your office and ask them for their opinion. Ask them how you've improved, ask them in which ways you've improved, and ask them how you can do better. Get updated feedback from coworkers, and if you need to set a new goal, then set one. Re-institute your goals, take the feedback seriously, and put it to action.

Case study. As I had planned when I set my CLEAR goals, a useful way for me to understand whether or not I was following through properly was to do weekly check-ins with my coworkers for an entire month. I took these check-ins very seriously, and I wanted my coworkers' honest feedback.

During the first week or two, I didn't really notice much difference in the way people acted around me. Many coworkers still avoided me, I wasn't invited to hang out with anyone after work, and some people still tended to tune out things I said at meetings. When I did check-ins, however, I understood that it would take time for people to accept that I was working on fixing my toxic behavior. People wouldn't change their negative perceptions of me overnight, and that's okay.

When I checked in with my coworkers again about halfway through the month, however, they said that they saw a noticeable difference in the way I was interacting with people and how I carried myself. Toward the end of the month, I personally noticed a complete shift. People started to have more in-depth conversations with me throughout the workday, and no one seemed to be actively avoiding me anymore. Everyone generally seemed to feel more comfortable around me. I even got invited to a happy hour that last week of the month. I decided to go, and we all discussed the noticeable changes I had made.

All of my coworkers were in agreement, and they were all very receptive to the "new me." It felt good to have the support of my coworkers and to have them acknowledge the work I did to get to that point. I knew that this was something I would continuously work on—well beyond my month-long goal. I'm glad I was able to make this change—not just for my benefit, but for the benefit of my entire team and my company as well.

It's one thing to talk about other people who are jerks at work, but it's really important to also look at yourself. Don't assume that you're perfect, because you probably aren't. I don't think there is a single person on this planet who is perfect. All of us generally engage in bad behaviors at work, and it's in our best interest to make sure that we identify those bad behaviors and take action to neutralize them.

10

HIRE SLOW, FIRE FAST

*You can't run a popularity contest
and be successful.*

—ARA PARSEGHIAN

If you're a manager, you are in a unique position when it comes to dealing with jerks at work. First of all, you have the ability to prevent most jerks from becoming a part of your organization by taking the time to really vet them in the hiring process. You are the one who hires, the one who interviews, and the one who makes decisions about these people.

While you're in the process of hiring or recruiting, you should be actively looking out for the signs of toxicity in potential employees. It can be difficult to get references from some former employers, but it usually is possible. To pick the best candidates, you must make sure that you do everything you can do to not hire someone who shows signs of being a potential office jerk. Of course, it can be difficult to pick up on signs after your first interaction with someone, but there are steps that you can take. These steps will force you to go the extra mile so that you will actively prevent the possibility of hiring someone who would be toxic to your workplace.

Be aware that you have the ability to prevent those people from becoming a part of your organization. And when you have got an irreconcilable jerk on your team, don't hesitate to counsel and coach them—and if necessary, to show them out the door. As a manager, you also have the ability and authority to ensure that if someone is acting like a jerk at work that they are counseled. You need to go above and beyond in order to fix any toxic behavior that may be happening in your office.

Ultimately, if the person can't correct their behavior, you should fire them. Remove people who aren't aligned with your organization's positive culture. The performance of your organization—and the morale and performance of your team—will improve immediately when you do.

To ensure that as a manager you are in full control of the situation throughout the hiring and firing process, there are five steps you can take. By following these steps, you will likely make fewer mistakes in the hiring process and avoid having to fire employees who may be exhibiting toxic behaviors.

1. TAKE YOUR TIME WHEN YOU HIRE

Many managers and others in charge of the hiring process tend to not spend enough time working through it—they tend to be in a big rush. In my own personal experience, the best managers really take their time to get to know each candidate better before they take the plunge and make an offer to hire them. This takes a lot of time—if you do it too quickly, chances are it will not be done well. So, when you take the time to get to know your candidates better up front, then there's a good chance that you'll be able to tell up front whether or not that person is going to be toxic. If you pick up on behavior in a job candidate that has you concerned, reference the field guide in Chapter 2 and see what kind of person you're dealing with.

Reaching out to other people as references is an important part of the process. Some organizations won't give you much feedback about the employee, however—in most cases because they're afraid they'll be sued by the candidate if they say anything bad about their performance or behavior. I've found that many times you can get candidate assessments from the person's manager, especially if that person has been a troublesome employee.

If they won't tell you outright that this person exhibits bad behavior in the workplace, they'll often give you hints along the way. You can kind of read between the lines what they're saying without them specifically having to say that the person you're about to interview is a bad person. In fact, if you ask them the simple question, "Would you hire this person again?" they may say that no, they wouldn't. That's all you need to know.

Another thing that you should always do is review your job candidate's social media. Take a look at their LinkedIn, Facebook, Twitter, Instagram, TikTok, and other social media to get an indication of what kind of person the candidate really is. Some people of course sanitize their social media when they're looking for a job and try to make themselves appear different than they really are. But many don't bother—they don't have any problem letting it all hang out. And when you find a long trail of negative posts and comments in a candidate's social media, you've got an early warning that this person may not be the best one to hire. So, take your time when you're in the hiring process.

Case study. As the manager of my team, I pride myself in taking hiring very seriously. I take my time getting to know the candidate in different ways. A few months ago, I was conducting an interview for a position in our office. I wanted to get an outside perspective from someone who had worked with the person in a professional work environment before, so I reached out to his previous employer. It took a few days, but the candidate's former boss eventually called me back. The boss was super vague about the candidate's behavior and she didn't say anything that was particularly helpful to me. She wasn't raving about him, but she also wasn't saying anything negative.

I finally decided to cut right to the chase, asking, "Would you hire him again?" She said no. That is all of the information I really needed to know, and the candidate had one strike against him—a big red flag.

Based on that answer, I wanted to understand the candidate in greater detail before I made my final assessment and decision. So, I took a look at the candidate's social media. In some ways, this is like a background search that usually shows the person's true self. Some of the things I found on this specific candidate's Facebook page were shocking. There was no way I would want someone like that in my office. He used racial and gender slurs in several posts that would definitely not bode well on my team. This to me was another big red flag, and a sign that this person would most likely exhibit their social media behavior in the workplace once they were hired.

By taking the time to do background checks, and really getting to know the person in the interview and outside of the interview, I knew that this person would not be a good fit for the job, and I didn't even bother scheduling an interview.

2. INTERVIEW, INTERVIEW, INTERVIEW

The interview process is a great opportunity for you to get to know the candidate better. This is a part of the hiring process where you should spend a lot of time, and not just rush through it. Instead of just one interview with you, it's much better to schedule multiple interviews with this person—both with yourself and with others on your team. I've personally found that the most successful organizations are the ones that have three or more interviews scheduled—not with just one interviewer but with several.

For example, some of the organizations that I've interviewed with in the past required multiple interviews. I went through four or five different interviews with different people in the organization, all asking different kinds of questions. You might, for example, have several interviews scheduled over the course of a morning—one after another. Or you could have a group interview with a team of people interviewing this person all at once. Each person who conducts an interview will be able to provide interesting feedback that you may not have realized yourself.

Involve employees and team members in the interviewing process. Their insight is invaluable, and they may be able to pick up on toxic behaviors that they've had to deal with in the workplace before.

Again, interview, interview, interview, and take your time. Schedule multiple interviews not just with yourself, but with others in the office. Gather all of their feedback together and find out what people think. Are people gung ho for this candidate or do they have reservations? If they have reservations, what are those reservations? What do you think the problems might be once this employee is hired? Listen to the others interviewing—their observations and opinions on potential hires are important.

Case study. When I make a new hire, I work directly with HR at our company and initially select the candidates that I like the best based on the cover letters and resumes they send in. I usually will let the HR do an initial interview, and then I'll do my own one-on-one interview with the candidate. This worked great for quite some time, but I felt that there was more I could do to ensure that I could avoid hiring the wrong person for our team—someone who was toxic. I've made a few mistakes in the past and wanted to see what I could do better in the hiring process.

Recently, we had an entry-level position that we were hiring for, and I decided that I wanted to include more people from our team in the hiring process this time. From my previous experiences of accidentally hiring people who later proved to not be a good fit for our office, I realized that since my employees would be the ones working closest with the new hire, they should have a say. I decided to plan multiple interviews for each of the candidates, and a few people from the team would be my interviewers. The final interview the candidate would have would be with me.

This process really worked well for us, and I could tell that my team appreciated having their opinions heard. After each day of interviewing, we would all debrief on each other's thoughts regarding the candidates up for the position. It was really helpful to hear everyone's feedback, and it made me understand each candidate much better. I felt I was able to get a better perspective on each candidate by having others interview rather than when it was just me conducting the interviews. Although the process took longer and required more time with each applicant, it was extremely helpful for choosing the best possible candidate.

3. HIRE FOR ALIGNMENT

Every company has its own unique culture. Every company has its own vision, its own mission, its own core values. And when you hire, you want to hire people who are aligned with those core values, mission, and vision of your organization. This means they are aligned with your company and office culture.

If, for example, you have a very formal company culture where people are dressed up for client meetings, or if your business is very rigid and highly regimented, then you'll want to hire people who like that kind of environment. Preferably these people are used to working in a culture that has similar or the same values that you share. You don't want someone who doesn't match the values of your office because they will just not work out.

While in the hiring process with people, you'll want to feel that out whether or not a person aligns with your company and office values and culture. You'll want to understand if the potential hire is going to be the kind of person who will fit in well when you hire them. Are they going to be aligned with your culture, your mission, your vision, your core values?

On the flip side, you also don't want to hire a really rigid person if your organization is agile, fast moving, and informal—it just may not be the best match. It's important to get a feel for whether or not the person is going to be aligned with your culture, and everything else that matters to your team and company. Try to avoid hiring people who are clearly unaligned with those important factors. Make sure to take your time with hiring, and really get a feel for whether the alignment is there or not.

Case study. Our office culture is particularly more laid back, and we tend to periodically work crazy hours. I know that it is not a job for everyone, but many people thrive in the environment. When hiring, I decided to write out the key characteristics of our office culture so that the rest of the interviewers and I could reference it while interviewing. The characteristics I came up with were: open minded, energized, long days, nonconventional hours, often work from home, informal, friendly, enthusiastic, passionate about what we do.

As we all reconvened to talk about each candidate, we would go through the list to see if the candidate fit our company culture. While doing this, we were able to cross a few people off the list because we realized that they might just be too rigid and formal to fit in with our team. We needed people who would get along with the rest of the employees and who would be aligned with and supportive of our team's culture. This was helpful to think about in the hiring process, and it narrowed down the list of candidates for us.

4. CORRECT, COUNSEL, AND COACH

You're never going to know absolutely 100 percent about the person you're hiring and whether or not the person is going to turn out to be a jerk at work and be toxic for the team. We can usually avoid this outcome if we do our due diligence with each candidate, but there are always people who slip through the cracks by masking their toxic behavior well during the hiring process. In all reality, you won't really know until you hire them whether or not they will be the perfect match.

So, what then? That's where you'll need to correct, counsel, and coach. Correcting an employee means to provide them with immediate feedback about some negative behavior. When someone engages in a toxic behavior, you need to correct them immediately. That means verbally dealing with the issue right then and there. If the behavior is toxic or bad, call it out right away. Don't let it go on, and don't let it fester. Correct your employee so that other people in the office do not become victims to the bad behavior.

Counseling is a bit more formal. It's where you actually call an employee into your office and provide them with more formal counseling, which may actually end up in their employee file depending on how you handle it. Point out the toxic behavior you've observed, explain the negative impact of their behavior on the organization, and then tell them that they are not to engage in that behavior again. If they continue to do whatever they're doing, then you'll have to take further action, which may include letting that person go. Make sure that they're aware of the consequences.

Coaching is a very supportive activity for your employees, and you should engage in it regularly. When you think about a coach for a sports team, their job is to provide team members with training in the skills they need to succeed, along with unleashing the motivation that athletes need to succeed. That's exactly what many employees need as well. They need that positive coaching. They need to have examples, and they need to be coached through what it's like to be a good employee, to behave well and not engage in negative, toxic behaviors.

Case study. As most managers do at some point or another, I have accidentally hired a few people who ended up not being the best employee and coworker. Some people are harder to pinpoint in the hiring process, and it isn't until they start working in your office that you begin to realize their toxic behaviors.

Last year, I hired someone new to our office. She was great in the interviewing process, and everything about her seemed perfect. It wasn't until a few months after I hired her that a few of my employees took me aside to tell me that they were having issues with the new hire. She would complain about everything and anything—almost constantly. She complained about our work processes and said we weren't as efficient as her former office. She complained about the way our office was laid out. She complained about the hours we worked. She complained about the work she had to do for her job. And on and on.

It was getting on my nerves, as well as others', and I decided to pull her into my office to discuss her behavior. I went through the steps: correct, counsel, and coach. The first time I spoke to her, I told her about the concerns I had with her behavior, and that it would be greatly appreciated if she could work on complaining less. She seemed to take it well and said that she would do better.

A week went by, and nothing seemed to change. I decided to have a more formal meeting with her in my office to counsel her on the behavior she was exhibiting. I told her that I had noticed her partaking in her bad behavior again, and that it was causing negative implications within the office. Her complaining was causing others to have lowered morale and a reduction of overall happiness while at work. I was hopeful that she would understand how harmful her behavior was by explaining how her actions were causing problems for our company as a whole.

Another week went by, and there was no noticeable difference, and people in the office were still coming to me to discuss their annoyance with her. This was my final straw. I brought her back into my office to coach her. I told her different ways that she could go about not being so pessimistic, and I restated that she needed to stop complaining about everything. If she spun things in a positive light, it would be beneficial to her overall mindset at work. I also instructed her that whenever she had the urge to complain about something in front of other coworkers, she should write it down rather than say it out loud.

We went through different methods she could use to fix her toxic behavior, and she agreed to try them out in order to disengage her negative thoughts and actions. It was great to go through each of these steps because it gave her the opportunity to identify and then change her behavior.

5. FIRE AS A LAST RESORT

Some people are unfortunately just not going to improve. They just won't get better, no matter how much you try to help them. Some people are toxic through and through, and you've got to deal with that. As a manager, it's your job to try to help that person, but if they can't be helped—and if they aren't interested in being helped for whatever reason—you need to take action.

I don't think many managers enjoy firing people, but sometimes they need to do it because the person is being toxic to the workplace. They're poisoning other employees and they're causing good people to look for other jobs. If you tolerate someone who is being toxic in the workplace, your employees will lose respect for you because they're going to wonder why you are tolerating the bad behavior. Why are you letting this person skate on through without challenging them? Why should the employees who are not partaking in negative behaviors bother being a good employee when apparently you don't care about someone behaving poorly? You will lose the respect of those employees in many cases, and they'll start looking for other jobs.

Recall the research conducted by Gallup that revealed that bad bosses are the number one reason people leave their jobs. If you aren't dealing with bad behavior in the office, then you're going to find that some of your best employees are going to start looking for other employment opportunities and they may leave as a result.

The other aspect of firing people is that it's really in the best interest of the employee who is being fired. If they aren't aligned with your culture, if it's just not working out, then it's not doing *them* any good being a part of your organization. If they're being triggered to engage in toxic behavior, it may be because they aren't happy in your organization.

There are many people who I know from my own experience as a manager who grouse about their jobs and say, "I wish I could work anywhere else but this place." Well, as a manager, you have the ability to help them along their way.

If they don't like working at your organization and with your team, then by all means, show them the door. They shouldn't be there. Firing the toxic employee will be the best thing—not only for your team, but for your company, your customers, and also for that employee who is clearly unhappy with their job.

Case study. A few weeks after I coached the toxic employee about how to disengage from her toxic behavior of complaining, nothing seemed to improve. She seemed to engage in this behavior less in front of me, but she was clearly still partaking since other coworkers mentioned to me that she wasn't improving.

After going through the previous steps with her, that was all I could really do to help. I couldn't let her continue in the position at our office if it was hurting the rest of the coworkers and causing them to feel uncomfortable at work. Also, I felt that if she was complaining about her job and our office so much, she might be able to find a better job for her elsewhere. Maybe our office wasn't a good fit for her, and she was just unhappy being a part of it.

I decided to fire her. When we had our termination meeting, I explained to her that she wasn't improving her negative behavior and that I had to look out for the well-being and productivity of the rest of the team. I also explained that it was my sincere hope that this action would be beneficial to her, and that I hoped she would be able to find a job that fit her best. I don't particularly like firing employees, but sometimes it's necessary for all involved.

Remember: when you hire people, take your time doing it. Get to know the candidates and don't rush the process, no matter how busy you are. The more rush you put into the process, the less you will get to know about the prospective employees and the greater the possibility of you hiring someone who will be toxic for other employees in your office. When you do identify a toxic person in the workplace who slipped through the cracks during the hiring process, correct the situation, counsel the employee, and coach them through it. But if things cannot be turned around for that employee, and nothing seems to be getting better, then don't hesitate to fire that person. It will not only be beneficial to your entire office, but for the employee exhibiting the bad behavior as well. It's a win-win all around.

THE MOST UNIQUE METHODS TO GET YOURSELF TO STOP PROCRASTINATING

Do you fall prey to procrastination? If so, you're not alone.

Research shows that over 20 percent of the population is affected by procrastination, and according to some studies, procrastination has more than quadrupled in the last thirty years. Among students, procrastination is especially pervasive, with some surveys revealing that 85 to 95 percent of students have procrastination-related problems. For those in the workforce, statistics also suggest that 40 percent of people have experienced a financial loss due to procrastination.[9]

There is a wide variety of reasons we put things off. But at the same time, there are a lot of ways we can treat procrastination and complete tasks on time. Here are some suggestions from some businesspeople who have found ways to beat the procrastination habit once and for all.

Meditate

You can either cry about procrastination or do mental pushups. The actual mechanism is that meditation teaches awareness and control (also calm, but that doesn't matter for this use case).

—Tony Stubblebine, CEO and founder of Coach.me

Break Projects Down into Small Tasks with Cue Cards

Procrastinators fill their time with menial tasks because they provide immediate rewards. So, the secret to beating procrastination is devising a system to reward you whenever you act on the important things . . . . For example, if you're writing a book, break it into 500-word sections. Keep a stack of cue cards with notes on each section on one side of your computer. Every time you complete 500 words, flip that card face down on the other side. This reward gives you a shot of the feel-good hormone dopamine, pulling you through the process.

—Jonathan Goodman, founder of the Personal Trainer Development Center

Focus on the Feeling After Accomplishment

Whenever I'm unmotivated, I think about how I'm going to feel afterwards rather than how I feel in the moment. I ask myself: looking back from that place, what is the choice I know I must make?

—Katrina Ruth, founder and CEO of *The Katrina Ruth Show*

Put Yourself on a "Procrastination Diet"

Put yourself on a procrastination diet. Whenever you feel resistance, give yourself one task and then do it. Do two the next time, then three. The first few days of a diet can be hard, but it gets easier if you stick with it. Set aside an hour each day solely to be productive.

—Dottie Herman, CEO of Douglas Elliman

Think About How Your Procrastination Affects Others

I look at the total of my kids' four tuitions.

—Guy Kawasaki, chief evangelist at Canva (former chief evangelist at Apple)

ACKNOWLEDGMENTS

Thanks to my agent extraordinaire: Jill Marsal at Marsal Lyon Literary Agency. So great to continue to find cool books to work on together—let's do some more! And thanks to Michael Pye—associate publisher at Career Press—for deciding that just one book by Peter Economy wasn't enough.

Many thanks to the Career Press team who through their personal magic turned my not-exactly-perfect manuscript into the book you hold in your hands, including Jane Hagaman, designer and production editor Maureen Forys, and copyeditor Vanessa Ta.

Thanks also to my personal editor (and awesome daughter) Skylar Economy, who literally dragged the manuscript for this book kicking and screaming over the finish line. I couldn't have done it without your help!

And thanks to Jan—my wife, beach bum, and tiki drink partner (love you forever!)—and my remarkable sons Jackson and Peter. Looking forward to seeing what the future brings each one of you.

Oh. And thanks to Otava Yo—my favorite musical group at the moment—and to Kalliope, the ancient Greek chief of all muses, through which the words in my brain find their way into my books.

Last, but definitely not least, thanks to all the millions of people who have been clicking on my articles and reading my books—and those I've written for others—for all these many years. I owe each and every one of you the deepest debt of gratitude.

Long may you reign.

NOTES

1   Maeghan Ouimet, "The Real Productivity Killer: Jerks," *Inc. www.inc.com.*

2   Amy Adkins, "Millennials: The Job-Hopping Generation," *Business Journal,* Gallup.com, *www.gallup.com.*

3   Better Buys, "Employees Behaving Badly: What's really happening at the office?," Betterbuys.com, *www.better buys.com.*

4   Tom Nolan, "The No. 1 Employee Benefit That No One's Talking About," *Workplace,* Gallup.com, *www.gallup.com.*

5   Mary Abbajay, "What to Do When You Have a Bad Boss," *Harvard Business Review, www.hbr.org.*

6   Peter Economy, "LinkedIn Just Revealed the 4 Traits of Really Bad Bosses (and Here's How to Fix Them)," *Inc. www.inc.com.*

7   Captivate, Office Pulse, "Office Gossip Runs Rampant," *https://officepulse.captivate.com.*

8   Thomas S Bateman, DBA, "The Most Powerful Mindfulness Is Future-Focused," *Psychology Today, www.psychology today.com.*

9   Edward Lowe Foundation, "Stop Procrastinating," *Edward Lowe Foundation, https://edwardlowe.org.*

ABOUT THE AUTHOR

Peter Economy is a *Wall Street Journal* best-selling business author, ghostwriter, developmental editor, and publishing consultant with more than one hundred books to his credit (and more than three million copies sold). He has written columns on leadership and management for Inc.com (*The Leadership Guy*) and served for eighteen years as Associate Editor for *Leader to Leader* magazine, published by the Frances Hesselbein Leadership Forum. Peter taught MGT 453: Creativity and Innovation as a lecturer at San Diego State University, is on the National Advisory Council of The Art of Science Learning, and is a founding board member of SPORTS for Exceptional Athletes.

A graduate of Stanford University (with majors in Economics and Human Biology), Peter has worked closely with some of the nation's top business, leadership, and technology thinkers, including Jim Collins, Frances Hesselbein, Barry O'Reilly, Peter Senge, Kellie McElhaney, Jeff Patton, Marshall Goldsmith, Marty Cagan, Lolly Daskal, Guy Kawasaki, Emma Seppala, William Taylor, Jim Kilts, Jean Lipman-Blumen, Stephen Orban, Ken Blanchard, and many others.

Visit Peter at:

www.petereconomy.com (Website)
www.inc.com/author/peter-economy (Inc.)
@bizzwriter (Twitter)